To Ali
Thank you for sharing
our love of the game,
and Charles Boy
Blae Herd
6/21/2015

In Partnership With

America's St. Andrews

Linking golf from its past to its future,
publicly-owned Chambers Bay is the dream realized

Foreword by
Robert Trent Jones Jr.

BY BLAINE NEWNHAM
EDITED BY TOM CADE

www.AmericasStAndrews.com

ISBN: 978-0-9960688-0-2

Library of Congress Control Number: 2014941708

St. Andrews is used in the title of this book with the expressed written permission of St. Andrews Links Trust, the charitable organization which manages the seven public golf courses in St. Andrews, Scotland. Creating golf's future by honoring its past, St. Andrews Links Trust is dedicated to keeping the game available and open to all.

Author: Blaine Newnham
Editor & Publisher: Tom Cade
Art Director & Designer: Marilyn Esguerra

Printed in the USA by Walsworth Print Group

Published by Green Cloud Media
22905 7th Ave SE, Bothell, Washington 98021, United States of America

Green Cloud media

Dedication

BRIAN LANKER

1947-2011

How do you say thanks to someone who is gone? You do what he or she would have done had they been here. Not with as much grace and creativity, certainly, but with great appreciation.

One of the world's great photojournalists, Brian saw in Chambers Bay, as he did with his epic book, "I Dream a World," a story told in words as well as photographs.

He reminded us often that it wasn't about sunsets and silhouettes, but about telling a story. No one could do both better, however.

During the last two weeks of his life, he spent what precious little energy he had to ask questions and give answers about this book. We only wish he were here to enjoy the U.S. Open and the book we dedicate to him for his insight and inspiration.

The transformation of an abandoned
gravel pit into a community asset
capable of hosting the world....

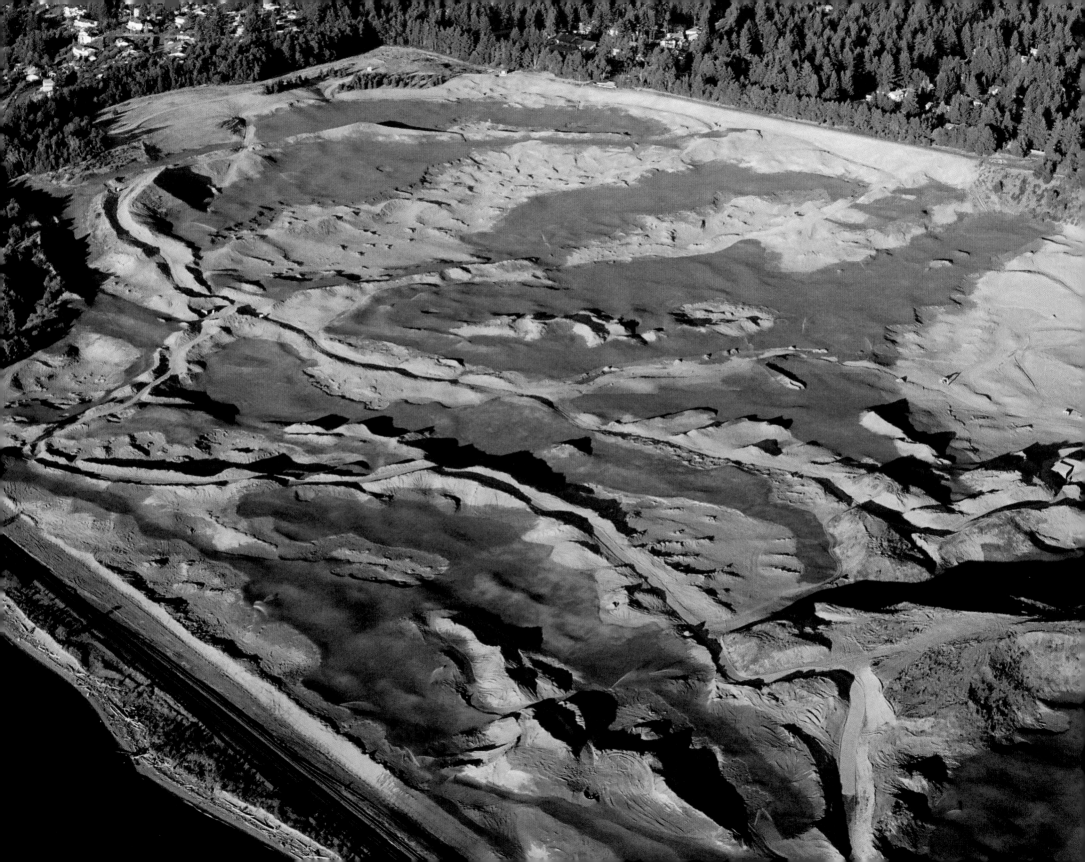

Table of Contents

Foreword

IN JUNE OF 1961 I MADE MY FIRST PILGRIMAGE to play the Old Course at St. Andrews a day after I arrived from America on my first European visit. I've been returning ever since and am honored to be a member of the Royal & Ancient Golf Club, whose clubhouse overlooks the first tee and 18th green. St. Andrews is still, and always will be, the true spiritual home of our game. I've come to know the Old Course intimately through study, play, and even a whisky-fortified walk of the bunkers.

When I was given the rare opportunity to create an authentic and original links course for Pierce County in Washington as part of a regional park I saw it as a gift from the golfing gods – those same gods that have kept watch over St. Andrews for the past 500 years.

I used the sandy soil hard by Puget Sound to craft a course at Chambers Bay that emphasizes strategic use of the ground game. We designed the layout to challenge local golfers as well as the most skilled touring pros who will face the course's defenses at the 2015 U.S. Open. Chambers Bay is the first new, original venue to be chosen by the USGA to host its Open Championship since they chose my father's work at Hazeltine National in Minnesota in 1970.

The events surrounding the selection of Chambers Bay for our national Open are beautifully chronicled by Blaine Newnham in the pages that follow. It's a compelling story of how a passionate, dedicated team of golfers all came together at the perfect time to create a venue worthy of hosting our national championship while simultaneously offering the public the opportunity to make Chambers Bay their own.

Chambers Bay is alive with the spirit of St. Andrews – a true links course open to everyone that's also good enough to attract and challenge the greatest players in the world.

Blaine's book is a keepsake that celebrates our ancient game in its modern context. I know you'll enjoy the pages that follow as much as you'll love playing Chambers Bay.

Robert Trent Jones Jr

Introduction

IN UNDERSTANDING THE NEWNESS OF CHAMBERS BAY, the place to begin is in the past.

How can we possibly put this untested layout, still in its infancy, in the same conversation with St. Andrews, the home of golf? They both are brown and salty fescued links courses, yes, but more than that they are both publicly owned and publicly used, by pilgrims seeking a world-class golf experience and by neighborhood families out for an evening stroll through the property. Their property.

Chambers Bay, like St. Andrews, is a local gathering place, a park, a trail, a vista, a destination. It allows access not only to the course, but to a beach and a grassy amphitheater.

It is in some ways already iconic. Indeed, the cement holding pens that remain along the 18th fairway are relics of Tacoma's mighty industrial past, a "Northwest Stonehenge." The Lone Fir that stands beside the 16th teeing ground is immediately recognizable in any photo of the course.

So let's talk about it as "America's St. Andrews," and how the same kind of foresight that put aside land in the middle of Manhattan for Central Park, or the best parts of the American wilderness for national parks, occurred at Chambers Bay, not as a wilderness area, but as a distinctly Puget Sound place to be and play.

Its use is as diverse as family picnics along the beach to the world's most demanding golf tournament, America's national championship.

The dream was not only to bring the U.S. Open to the Pacific Northwest for the first time in history, but to bring it every 10 years or so, placing Chambers Bay in the company of Shinnecock Hills, Merion, Pebble Beach and Bethpage as regular venues.

To create a course for the ages, one that will age well like a good single malt Scotch, be better 100 years from now than it is today, but always a public place, for kite-flying contests, road runs, beach walks, strolls along its rim with those crystalline views of the Olympic Mountains.

In laying out the course, the architects of Chambers Bay drew inspiration not from the pre-fabricated designs of the modern school, but from the wild and ancient – and unforgettable – courses of Scotland and Ireland.

Unlike many of the world's famous layouts that have held major championships, which are most times off limits, hidden behind forbidding walls, Chambers Bay and St. Andrews are always open, to golfers and non-golfers alike. One can walk through the middle of the course when golfers are playing, and when they aren't. Any time of day, you can walk over and have your picture taken on the Swilcan Bridge at St. Andrews, or near the trunk of Chambers Bay's Lone Fir.

St. Andrews and Chambers Bay share fescue grasses, and rumpled greens, and sand everywhere. They share wind off the water, fairways that are fast as greens, caddies, and the ethos of a walking-only experience.

But mainly they share openness. Nothing secret, nothing secluded, just golf and the elements.

The way it was, and the way, fortunately, it is. ✳

Chambers Bay, like St. Andrews,
is a local gathering place, a park,
a trail, a vista, a destination.

The Old Course at St. Andrews has been used for public events for centuries. In 1871, a woman pushes a baby carriage on the pathway behind the first tee and 18th green (upper left); and in 1901, the townspeople tested a new fire engine beyond the first green (lower left). It is a longstanding tradition that the course is closed to golfers on Sundays, leaving it open and available for walkers, picnickers, and those who want to get married on the Swilcan Bridge.

Golf at Chambers Bay is just one of the activities that are available on the Chambers Creek Properties.

The property's Central Meadow is used for nearly 20 corporate events each year, for concerts, as a venue for outdoor cinema, for high school cross-country track meets, and an annual kite festival. There is a playfield in the North Meadow, and off-leash pet areas. There is a three-mile long walking trail that winds around and through the golf course that is open to all, and at all times.

The land is used. The land is loved.

"To think that we could have an Open in the Northwest on a course next to the water and built on sand and with fescue grasses. It was a staggering proposition."

CHAPTER 1

The Decision

WE BEGIN ON THAT DAY IN FEBRUARY 2008, just eight months after the first tee shot was struck at Chambers Bay. "It was like winning the Oscar," said Bruce Charlton, president and chief design officer of the golf architecture firm Robert Trent Jones II. "Twice."

The United States Golf Association had selected Chambers Bay, a controversial municipal facility in University Place, a careworn suburb of Tacoma, Wash., to host the U.S. Amateur in 2010 and the U.S. Open in 2015. No course built in the past 45 years had been deemed worthy of holding our national championship, let alone one that had barely opened its doors.

One that was also a muni, had a Euro-brown look about it, and was located in the Northwest corner of the country.

The USGA was far too traditional, too crusty, too unimaginative to make such a choice.

Wasn't it?

In the 20th century and before, America's golf championship had been conducted at established private country clubs, great courses like Oakmont and Baltusrol, Winged Foot and Merion; most of them in the East, all of them exclusive.

In a quest to make the Open more egalitarian and utilize larger, public spaces, the USGA took a gamble in 2002 on the sprawling Bethpage State Park's Black Course, and the riotous New York galleries had given the Open a new, more vibrant feel.

Bethpage, the first true public course to hold an Open, hosted it again in 2009. Yes, it was pure public – with golfers waiting in their cars all night to get a spot on the tee sheet – but it was also built during golf's Golden Age of architecture and by one of the great designers, A.W. Tillinghast.

In other words, it had history.

Pebble Beach and Pinehurst, also selected to host Opens, allowed public play, certainly, but only at the price of a firstborn.

The West Coast had long been ignored by the USGA. No Opens were played in the West during its first 50 years. Finally, the championship was staged at Riviera Country Club near Los Angeles in 1948, and over the next 50-plus years came four times to the Olympic Club in San Francisco and four times to Pebble Beach.

Only in the 21st century did the Open become really open as Torrey Pines in San Diego followed the experiment at Bethpage and proved a great site for Tiger Woods' epic playoff win in 2008.

Still, there had never been an Open played in the Pacific Northwest. The PGA of America conducted a successful championship among the statuesque firs at Sahalee Country Club outside Seattle in 1998, but then reneged on its promise to return there in 2010. Sahalee was deemed not big enough for the modern major, and the PGA of America cast its lot instead with the monstrous Whistling Straits course in Wisconsin.

Would it be, could it be, that the only other major golf championships ever played in the Northwest were the wartime, 1944 PGA Championship at obscure Manito Golf and Country Club outside Spokane and the same event two years later at Portland Golf Club?

Certainly, Pumpkin Ridge, a marvelous 36-hole golf complex west of Portland, had deserved a shot at a U.S. Open. It had done the USGA's requisite apprenticeship, hosting two U.S. Women's Opens and a stirring U.S. Amateur won by Woods, plus various junior championships, and drawn great crowds.

Sahalee Country Club outside of Seattle was the site of the 1998 PGA Championship. Although the major was deemed a success and was scheduled to return there in 2010, it was decided by the PGA of America that it needed a larger venue and so canceled its return engagement. Instead, Sahalee hosted the 2010 U.S. Senior Open. Pictured is the par-3 17th hole during the 1998 championship.

Prior to the final match at the 1946 PGA Championship held at Portland Golf Club, Robert Hudson (center), a successful grocer from Portland who sponsored the championship, posed with finalists Ben Hogan (left) and Ed Oliver (right). Hogan would defeat Oliver in the match to take the title. The last year that the PGA Championship was contested in a match play format was 1957.

Hudson is known as the man who saved the Ryder Cup. The matches had not been held since 1937 because of World War II, so Hudson came forward to personally fund the British team and offered up Portland Golf Club as the venue in 1947. Hudson was the perfect host, meeting the British team in New York after they arrived on the Queen Mary and joining the players for the three-day rail journey to the Pacific Northwest.

Hudson was named the 1947 "Man of the Year" by the Golf Writers Association of America, and in 1953 served as president of the Pacific Northwest Golf Association. He was inducted into the Pacific Northwest Golf Hall of Fame in 1978.

On June 13, 2008, inside the USGA hospitality room during the second round of the U.S. Open being held at Torrey Pines in San Diego, the agreement was signed for Chambers Bay to be the site of the 2015 U.S. Open. At the table that day were (left to right) Robert Trent Jones Jr.; David Fay, who was then the executive director of the USGA; Pierce County Executive John Ladenburg; and Jim Vernon, the president of the USGA in 2008-09. Standing in the back were Jay Blasi (left) and Bruce Charlton, the on-site architects of Chambers Bay for the Jones team.

Muirfield in Gullane, Scotland has been the site of many British Opens, being a regular venue in the Open rota. The Open Championship was first held at Muirfield in 1892, just nine months after it opened. Pictured above is Muirfield's par-3 13th hole.

But the USGA was less concerned about the turnout than what it would do with that turnout. The facility had infrastructure problems. Its better course, Witch Hollow, simply lacked the room to move crowds around environmentally sensitive areas near the finishing holes. A plan to use the best holes of the two courses was rejected.

Was there any place else?

Enter Ron Read, a venerated USGA official, who took the trouble to look among the rubble of a depleted sand and gravel mine near Tacoma and see what Robert Trent Jones Jr. was talking about.

Jones had convinced Pierce County officials that he understood their dream of building a golf course that would transcend local play and players, a course that could become a magnet for tourism and economic development and could draw unprecedented attention to the Tacoma area.

A course that would endure.

Over the years, so many courses had been built with the intent of playing host to a U.S. Open. The last one to fulfill the dream, however, was Hazeltine National in Minnesota, built in 1962 by Jones' father. It garnered the first of its Open championships in 1970.

The younger Jones understood USGA politics, and he had the connections Pierce County needed to begin what they believed was a legitimate run at eventually staging the U.S. Open at Chambers Bay.

Jones called Read, who lived in Monterey, Calif. Jones and Read had been friends for over 40 years, and Read, who at the time was the director of the west region in the USGA hierarchy, had long supported the idea of playing the Open in the Northwest.

"I was what you call an early racer," Read said. "I raced up to see Bandon Dunes when it was just an idea, and I raced up to see Chambers Bay."

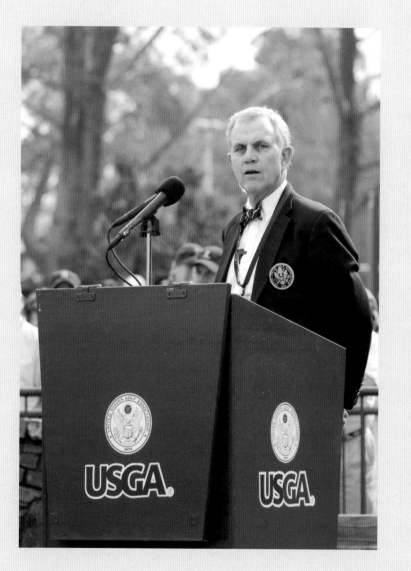

I call your name

As the first tee announcer at the U.S. Open for 22 consecutive years, Ron Read made more than 6,000 player introductions. To the audiences hanging outside the ropes, his "Play away, please" in sending the players down the first fairway was as lyrical as "Gentlemen, start your engines" is at Indianapolis.

Inside the ropes, however, Read was all business. He had a hand in just about everything while at the USGA, from the conception of the Slope rating in the handicap system to the decision to play the U.S. Open at Chambers Bay.

Read, the former USGA director of regional affairs, west region, calls himself a facilitator. As the starter, he set the pace for an Open, calling nervous players to the tee, reminding them to count their clubs, wishing them good luck.

He is so well thought of in the golf community that he was invited to be a member of the Royal & Ancient Golf Club and said he'd be more than pleased if his final round was at St. Andrews, the home of golf.

He was also the one who took the call from Robert Trent Jones Jr. and agreed to take the USGA's first look at a sand and gravel pit on the shores of Puget Sound.

But he doesn't rate U.S. Open courses. "It's the Open, a privilege, and they are all good," he said.

Read, who first was asked to be the starter for the 1986 U.S. Open at Shinnecock Hills and then was the starter at every U.S. Open from 1989 to 2010, said he knew he wouldn't be on the job forever.

"Bringing the U.S. Open to the Northwest had always been one of my goals, always," said Read in the men's locker room at Pebble Beach Golf Links during the second round of the 2010 championship, his final as the starter.

If a U.S. Open were going to be held in the Pacific Northwest, it was not anyone's first guess that it would be staged on a very un-Northwest-looking layout.

Read liked what he saw, and gathered Mike Davis and David Fay, his USGA bosses. They all reveled in the possibilities of what Jones could build and they would reap.

Read likes links golf, he likes sandy soils, he likes the Northwest and he saw in Chambers Bay the possibility of holding the biggest Open in history.

"The stars were aligned in 2002 at Bethpage," said Read. "Now, at Chambers, the galaxies could be aligned."

Chambers Bay might not have been the Northwest's last chance to secure an Open, but Read clearly was running out of alternatives.

Over the years he had taken looks at Peter Jacobsen's Oregon Golf Club, at Washington National south of Seattle, at The Reserve near Portland, at Newcastle in the hills above Bellevue, at TPC Snoqualmie Ridge 30 minutes east of Seattle, and, of course, at Pumpkin Ridge.

"Chambers Bay not only had the potential of a great course, but with the room for infrastructure, parking, corporate tents and galleries, it had as much potential as any course on the planet," he said. "I'm certain the Scots who have lent us this game, and the townspeople of St. Andrews, will be proud of Chambers Bay in 2015 and the Opens to come."

The odds against the nod going to a course that was less than a year old, however, were staggering. Just think of all the U.S. courses built since Hazeltine in 1962, courses by Dye and Nicklaus and Doak and Fazio, courses like Spyglass Hill, Whistling Straits, and Kiawah Island – only Chambers Bay, and later Erin Hills in Wisconsin (2017), were picked to hold U.S. Opens.

But the reasons behind the eventual selection of Chambers Bay began to emerge as early as the first visit by a USGA official, even before a shovel of sand had been turned on the 900 acres bordering Puget Sound.

"My gosh," said Davis, at the time the person most responsible for the USGA looking at new and different markets, "to think that we could have an Open in the Northwest on a course next to the water and built on sand and with fescue grasses. It was a staggering proposition." Davis had been the senior director of rules and competitions at the USGA before ascending to the association's executive director position in 2011.

The par-4 14th hole at Royal Dornoch in Scotland.

Links to the New World

Named in part for the view of Fox Island just across the water from Chambers Bay, the course's second hole is named "Foxy" also as an homage to the Scottish links course from which it draws its lineage. A plaque has been placed near the hole's teeing ground which reads: "Honoring the great links tradition of the Royal Dornoch Golf Club, in the Highlands of Scotland, with its outstanding 14th hole named Foxy. Dornoch has inspired generations of golfers and golf course architects, including the designers of Chambers Bay."

The plaque was donated through the Chambers Creek Foundation. Royal Dornoch was designed by Old Tom Morris in 1877.

From the beginning, Chambers Bay, the outrageous idea of Pierce County Executive John Ladenburg, wanted the USGA, and the USGA wanted Chambers Bay.

"We were good listeners," said Tony Tipton, then the project manager for Pierce County. "We did things with having the U.S. Open in mind."

In a sense, they designed the course together, making sure there were no reasons that the Open couldn't be contended there, and every reason that it should.

Give Pierce County officials credit for the vision. They, not the USGA, hired Robert Trent Jones Jr. to design the course and gave his team the money to move more than a million cubic yards of sand to create Turnberry in Tacoma.

"I told them they could have as much land and as big a budget as they needed," said Ladenburg. "We wanted to do something that could last 100 years."

There was the vision, and of course, the vicinity.

"You just don't find those conditions in an urban setting," said Ron Whitten, the architectural editor of *Golf Digest*.

Chambers Bay is 30 minutes from Sea-Tac International Airport, and only an hour from Seattle, with the real possibility of patrons disembarking at a temporary station near the 18th tee from dedicated trains arriving from King Street Station in downtown Seattle.

There were mountain and water views for television, benevolent weather for players, and, mostly, wide open spaces – room for corporate and media compounds, room for parking, room for as many as 50,000 spectators a day.

Clearly, the USGA was poised to pick Chambers Bay for something. But for what? And for when?

After losing the Whistling Straits course to the PGA of America for its championship and sincere in its hope to play the Open in the Northwest, the USGA wasn't to be denied this time by tradition or by anything else.

"I thought that we had a good chance to get a U.S. Amateur," said Ladenburg, "and depending how that went, a U.S. Open. I never, ever dreamed we would get both of them."

Ladenburg sent a letter applying for a U.S. Amateur. The 2010 date – just three years after Chambers Bay opened – came into play when Congressional Country Club in Maryland notified the USGA that it was having problems with its greens and would be unable to host the Amateur one year (2010) and the Open the next (2011).

Ladenburg waited through the first winter of operation for a USGA response. He heard, instead, from the PGA of America, expressing interest in holding its championship in the Northwest again.

Ladenburg demurred.

"This whole thing began with going after the U.S. Open and I wasn't going to do anything that might detract from that," he said.

The break for Chambers Bay came just before Christmas 2007 when a majority of the membership at the legendary Winged Foot Golf Club in New York said it had lost interest in its desire to hold the 2015 Open.

The USGA had other options, but here was a chance to wrap up Chambers Bay, to have the first Open not only in the Northwest, but the first played on fescue grasses in a gorgeous setting overlooking the waters and islands of Puget Sound and the snow-tipped mountains of the Olympics.

Ladenburg was asked to send one more letter.

"It's already in the mail," he said.

And so the story was unfolding, the story of a great reclamation project that transformed an ugly, weed-covered sand pit into a civic treasure. A story about dreaming the impossible dream and then realizing it, and about a new way to play a game that is older than the hills and fabulous dunes of Chambers Bay. ✳

The Time Had Come

Early on a winter's morning in January of 2009, a small cargo truck made its way down the path toward the putting green that sits next to the starter house at Chambers Bay. Three workers got out of the truck and within an hour had installed a 12-foot tall Rolex clock, the definitive and enduring symbol to all who walk past it heading for the first tee that championship golf is played here.

It was on that day and at that moment that it became real, became tangible, that the promise made by the USGA – that a U.S. Amateur and a U.S. Open would be contested on these fescue-covered dunescapes alongside Puget Sound – would indeed be fulfilled.

For the first time ever in the Pacific Northwest.

CC: Tony
Ron

United States Golf Association
Golf House, P.O. Box 708, Far Hills, NJ 07931-0708
T 908 234-2300   F 908 234-9687
www.usga.org

RECEIVED
MAR 27 2006
Pierce Co. Executive

March 23, 2006

Mr. John W. Landenburg
County Executive
Pierce County
930 Tacoma Avenue South, Room 737
Tacoma, WA 98402-2100

Dear John,

Now that I have finally gotten back to the office, I wanted to write to say how wonderfully impressed I was with the Chambers Bay Golf Course project. While it is too early to predict just how good the golf course will be and what the future may hold for tournament golf, I can say without qualification that you and Pierce County have the real possibility to hit a "homerun" with Chambers Bay.

As for the future of a USGA championship, including a U.S. Open, at this point I can not see any particular aspect that would hold Chambers Bay back. While it is very premature to comment on the golf course, Chambers Bay appears to have all the other things we are looking – it is in the Pacific Northwest; it is being built on sand (firm and fast conditions even with rain); its views being on the water are fabulous; it will be open to the public; it has more than ample space to allow for a large tournament's operations; and it seems to have the government and community backing for a large-scale event. The part that is the relative unknown at this point is the golf course. I get the sense that Bobby and his team are going to build a wonderful golf course, and a good test of golf.

I have already spoken to David Fay, USGA Executive Director, and several other senior staff about Chambers Bay. All are excited about the potential future. I plan to come back this summer on my way to the Curtis Cup Match at Bandon Dunes. I likely will be at Chambers Bay, assuming plans do not change, the afternoon of July 19.

Congratulations again John for having the vision and desire to start the Chambers Bay project. I truly hope things go along as smoothly as possible during the building phase. We are pleased that you have contacted us. In the meantime, please keep us apprised of the project's progress.

Have a great 2006.

Sincerely,

Mike Davis
Senior Director, Rules & Competitions

PW – Chambers Bay

Pierce County

Office of the County Executive
930 Tacoma Avenue South, Room 737
Tacoma, Washington 98402-2100
(253) 798-7477 • FAX (253) 798-6628

JOHN W. LADENBURG
Executive
jladenb@co.pierce.wa.us

LYLE QUASIM
Chief of Staff
lquasim@co.pierce.wa.us

March 28, 2006

Mike Davis, Senior Director, Rules & Competitions
United States Golf Association
Golf House
P O Box 708
Far Hills, NJ 07931-0708

Dear Mike:

Thanks for your nice letter about Chambers Bay. As the course comes together, we are getting more and more excited about the project and the possibility that it can become a nationally and internationally known venue. We are absolutely committed to making this a golf course that will stand the test of time and will be a world-class public site.

We appreciate your advice and help in making sure that this course is able to handle any kind of challenge, from the best of the professionals and amateurs, to the crowds and needs of a major championship. We realize that only a select few courses can achieve the highest status in a few short years, but we are prepared to do what it takes to bring championship golf to the Pacific Northwest, and to provide a venue that can be a challenge to the best players in the world.

You mention others, like Director Fay, whom you have told about the course. Please let them know that should they be in the area, we are prepared to give them a full tour. I can't promise Bobby can be here, but I can assure you that we want them to see the vision we have for this site. I have noted the July 19th date and put it on my calendar. If anyone in your organization who will be here earlier in July for the Gold Mountain championship would like a tour, we would be happy to set it up.

I am trying to find a date during the Public Links Championship when I can come up to Bremerton and spend a day watching how you present a championship. Would any particular day be best?

Again, thanks for the input on the course. We will keep you advised of our progress.

Sincerely,

John W. Ladenburg
Pierce County Executive

Office of the County Executive

930 Tacoma Avenue South, Room 737
Tacoma, Washington 98402-2100
(253) 798-7477 • FAX (253) 798-6628

JOHN W. LADENBURG
Executive
jladenb@co.pierce.wa.us

LYLE QUASIM
Chief of Staff
lquasim@co.pierce.wa.us

July 23, 2007

Mr. Mike Davis
Senior Director, Rules & Competitions
United States Golf Association
P.O. Box 708
Far Hills, NJ 07931-0708

Dear Mr. Davis:

Congratulations to you and the USGA on the recently held U.S. Open at Oakmont Country Club. It was truly a spectacular week of golf and an outstanding championship event.

While we would have enjoyed being there ourselves, we were, of course, busy with the opening of the Chambers Bay golf course. In every sense, it was a great success. A week of exciting events and an opening gala attended by more than 350 people led up to the first tee time early Saturday morning, June 23rd. The weather was perfect and, according to everyone who played, so was the golf. Indeed, word has spread quickly about Chambers Bay. Media reviews have been universally positive and extensive networking within the golf community has already resulted in more than 10,000 tee time reservations.

A project of the size and scope of Chambers Bay requires a talented team of individuals with true passion and commitment. Pierce County, Robert Trent Jones II and KemperSports have all worked hard to make Chambers Bay a course of distinction that will attract golf enthusiasts from around the region, the country and the world.

We are extremely pleased you and USGA staff members have been able to tour the course and we appreciated the helpful comments you made while the course was under construction, Mike. During your visits and subsequent discussions, we have become more convinced then ever Chambers Bay has what it takes to host a major golf championship. Others at the Washington and Pacific Northwest Golf Associations are equally excited about the opportunity.

With that in mind, we respectfully request the USGA consider bringing the U.S. Amateur Championship to Chambers Bay as early as 2011 and the U.S. Open Championship in 2016.

Pierce County would be proud to partner with the USGA and we stand ready to begin discussions at your earliest convenience. The Governor has personally told me of her support and willingness to partner to bring a championship to our State. Chambers Bay can offer the

Mr. Mike Davis
Senior Director, Rules & Competitions
July 23, 2007
Page 2

best golfers in the world a challenging but fair test of their skills in an environment unique to the United States. At the same time, Chambers Bay was specifically designed to handle the operational considerations necessary to hold a world-class championship. But most of all, the immediate popularity of Chambers Bay is proof the local community and the Pacific Northwest would enthusiastically support a USGA event in every conceivable way and work diligently to ensure its success.

On a related note, Chambers Bay will host two events this October featuring talented professionals and amateurs. First, the 2007 South Puget Sound Junior Clinic and Skins Game Charity Fund Raiser will be held October 9th. It will be a four player contest consisting of Ryan Moore, Michael Putnam, Aaron Baddeley and Bubba Watson. The second event is the Big Ten/Pac Ten Challenge scheduled for October 21st and 22nd. Eight teams will engage in tournament play over two days. Any assistance from the USGA in setting up the course for these two events would be greatly appreciated.

On behalf of Pierce County, the State of Washington and the entire Pacific Northwest region, allow me to say it would be an immense honor for a major USGA golf championship to be held at Chambers Bay. Please consider our request and don't hesitate to give me a call with any questions, concerns or comments.

Warm Regards,

John W. Ladenburg
Pierce County Executive

cc: James B. Hyler Jr., Chairman, USGA Championship Committee

The place was a mess, the industrial leftovers of 100 years of mining, a grisly landscape of gravel mounds, scrub trees and shallow drainage ponds.

CHAPTER 2

The Vision

TO UNDERSTAND THE PHENOMENON OF CHAMBERS BAY, you first need to understand John Ladenburg, who made a dream a destiny.

He asked why, if New York could bring the U.S. Open to Bethpage State Park, why Tacoma couldn't do it at Chambers Bay.

And then he audaciously answered the question almost by himself.

Ladenburg supplied the vision and the political will for the $24-million project called Chambers Bay. Without him, none of this would have happened.

A trial lawyer by profession, Ladenburg was a competitor by nature. It came with the territory which, as one of 16 children in a Tacoma family, meant not only survival, but recognition.

In the 1980s, he played on a slow-pitch softball team called "The Family," which was comprised of himself and his eight brothers, and attracted the attention of *Sports Illustrated*. Fittingly, Ladenburg played third base, the toughest position on a slow-pitch softball team, and had the broken fingers that went along with it.

He quit playing while in his 40s when he could no longer get out of bed after a multi-game tournament, just like he had quit skiing when he could no longer handle the most severe runs.

Ladenburg simply doesn't do anything halfway. Neither did his dad, a high-wire, high-voltage electrician.

The Ladenburgs have roots in the pioneer days of Tacoma, dating back to John's great-grandmother who settled there. He graduated from Stadium High, then Gonzaga University in Spokane, where he returned later to get a law degree.

A relentless prosecutor for the county following his election in 1986, he took on racketeering, sexual abuse, environmental tragedy and gang violence.

In 2000, with 60 percent of the vote, he became Pierce County Executive and was re-elected in 2004, giving him enough time and political currency to develop the fading sand and gravel mine in University Place.

The place was a mess, the industrial leftovers of 100 years of mining, a grisly landscape of gravel mounds, scrub trees and shallow drainage ponds.

Early in his tenure, Ladenburg walked the site, which had been purchased by the county in 1992.

"I was more impressed with the potential of the two miles of beach than anything else," he said. "The county had a 50-year plan for the area for some kind of recreational use. I wasn't sure what we needed to do but I knew that, whatever it was, it wouldn't take 50 years."

Above: One of 16 children, John Ladenburg (third from right) and his eight brothers had formed a slow-pitch softball team called "The Family" that eventually was the subject of a feature article in a national sports magazine. In a family that large, competition came with the territory.

There were lots of ideas. Hiking trails, an arboretum, a park, and, yes, a golf course. Because of its proximity to the county's water treatment plant, options were limited and none except golf had the potential to raise money as well as global awareness.

"Trying to maintain 300 acres of lawn isn't easy, and can be expensive," said Tony Tipton, the project manager at Chambers Bay during and after Ladenburg's tenure. "We all thought about a golf course, to be compatible with the water treatment plant and to take advantage of the western exposure and views of Puget Sound and the Olympic Mountains. We could eventually irrigate the course from reclaimed water from the treatment plant."

But what kind of golf course?

Ladenburg did his case preparation as county executive as if he were still the county prosecutor, researching everything about golf he could find.

He was enamored by John Feinstein's book, "Open – Inside the Ropes at Bethpage Black." It told the behind-the-scenes story of how the U.S. Open went from exclusive clubs to a New York State Park.

"I thought," Ladenburg said, "if New York can do it, why can't we do it."

"One hundred years from now," Ladenburg said, "they will still be playing golf at Chambers Bay, much as they are at St. Andrews in Scotland."

Standing on the rain-soddened floor of the abandoned gravel pit in 2004, the prospects of the property were not viewed as promising. The place was littered with old work sheds and the ruins of its industrial past. But the same view, 10 years later, reveals the 18th fairway as a living, breathing entity, and the ruins themselves have become starkly beautiful monolithic pieces of art.

From that point on, everything Ladenburg did was focused on getting the U.S. Open, even though he might have been happy with a PGA Tour event, or the U.S. Amateur or U.S. Senior Open.

It was unlikely the Open would ever come to University Place, but Ladenburg was uncompromising in his approach.

His research showed that only 49 courses had held U.S. Opens, that none built since 1962 was among them, that only Bethpage had been a true publicly-owned course, and that the odds against him were overwhelming.

"That is why we couldn't compromise on anything," he said. "I told our people, 'If we do 99 percent of the preparation right, we are not going to get a U.S. Open; we can't compromise on a single thing or we'll be eliminated from consideration.'"

Ladenburg rallied the troops.

He was criticized for strong-arming the county council, which he probably did.

First, he had to convince everyone that this wasn't just a golf course. There were plenty of good tracks in Pierce County for the average player, he told everyone. And he was right.

No, this was about economic development, and about a legacy.

"One hundred years from now," Ladenburg said, "they will still be playing golf at Chambers Bay, much as they are at St. Andrews in Scotland."

Then he began making his case that the course could be paid for by the players, not the taxpayers. He did economic study after economic study trying to prove that although the debt was $24 million for construction, in time it would be paid off and the course would return money to the county.

"We were considering it at a time when the county was flush," said Terry Lee, a council member who represented the University Place area. "None of us were golfers. We knew the site had to be reclaimed. And John, as always, was extremely persuasive. We all became true believers, but looking back and knowing what I know now, I'm glad we did."

In presenting his vision to Pierce County – to the council as well as to the county residents themselves – Ladenburg prepared his case with the same passion and preparation that he employed during his tenure as a county prosecutor. The local television network – the county-owned Pierce County TV – recorded most of the meetings at which the property, and the golf course project, was discussed. Ladenburg managed to win every 4-3 vote during the process, but at times the debates would get so heated that he would storm out of the meetings.

Ladenburg saw himself as a facilitator in the process of bringing the U.S. Open to Chambers Bay. His job, he felt, was to set the table and then get everyone to actually sit at the table. Before the course had even opened, Ladenburg was able to arrange site visits with USGA officials, particularly Mike Davis (above left) who, prior to becoming the USGA's executive director in 2011, was the association's senior director of rules and competitions, with one of his main duties being the setting up of U.S. Open courses.

And whenever possible, Ladenburg brought Davis together with Robert Trent Jones Jr. (above right), the golf course architect who had been hired for the job by Ladenburg.

It was Jones – and his chief design officer, Bruce Charlton – who was able to convince Ron Read to make a trip to the Northwest to see what was happening on the shores of Puget Sound. Read (in yellow hat on right, with Ladenburg, during a site visit a year before the course opened) was then a USGA director of regional affairs, and for years had been on the lookout for a course in the Northwest that could host a U.S. Open.

Lee admits that in leaner times the project might have come out looking entirely different.

"This was a time in history when something like this could be done, and we took advantage of it," he said.

Independent projections suggested that the course could produce enough revenue to pay off the bonds. These projections were done in the boom years approaching 2006. Chambers Bay opened in 2007, only to be crippled by the bust of 2008.

Through it all, the course continued to make money. Just not enough to cover the payments on the debt.

The county would have to make up the difference, looking long-range to better times when the debt had been paid off and the profits would go to other recreational-related initiatives.

All the while, through boom and bust, Ladenburg remained steadfast in his quest for the Holy Grail, a U.S. Open to bring headlines around the world to bear on Pierce County.

The property for the golf course was huge, covering the better part of 300 acres. You could easily put in 27 holes. At a time when golf was being assailed as too tough and too expensive, why not put in a good, solid 27 holes everyone could afford and enjoy?

Ladenburg, who had taken up golf a few years earlier, had different ideas.

He stopped the mining that had continued after the county had purchased the property in the early 1990s.

"If he hadn't," said Tipton, the project manager, "there might not have been enough sand left to do what the architects wanted."

The permit to continue mining remained after Glacier Northwest – the company that had quarried the property for years – concluded its work. When the course opened four years later, more than 1.5 million cubic

"There is this big meeting and John announces, 'We'll call the course Chambers Bay, we'll open in 2007 and we'll be walking.' Just like that."

On September 13, 2005, the Pierce County Council authorized the bonds to finance the construction of Chambers Bay. And 28 days later, on October 11, at 11:00 a.m. Pacific Daylight Time, the groundbreaking ceremony took place on a dusty plateau overlooking the 930-acre Chambers Creek Properties, of which nearly 300 acres would soon be molded into a links golf course with big plans.

Attending the ceremony, with golf clubs in hand, were (left to right) Valarie Zeeck, commissioner for the University Place Economic Development Task Force, and two-time president of the Chambers Creek Foundation; Shawn Bunney, Pierce County Council member; Pierce County Executive John Ladenburg; Terry Lee, Pierce County Council member; Ken Grassi, University Place Council member; and Bradley Bogue, who at the time was the president of the University Place Chamber of Commerce.

yards of sand had been moved, cleaned and sculpted to yield a course that was voted the "No. 1 New Course in the U.S." for 2007 by *Golf Digest* and quickly moved into the country's top-10 list of courses you can play.

Without the mining permit, the scope of the project might not have been nearly so grand. At one point, the architects who were chosen for the task of building a U.S. Open course, Robert Trent Jones II, said they might need more land, to which Ladenburg replied, "Use as much land and spend as much money as you need."

It was Ladenburg who had the final say in picking Jones as the architect.

"He better understood than the others what we wanted and how we could achieve it," Ladenburg said.

In the meantime, decisions had to be made.

What would the course be called, when would it open and, most importantly, would Ladenburg hang on to the dream of getting the Open even though it could mean sacrificing revenue?

First there was the issue of cart paths. Carts work for all but a few American courses, transporting players and producing revenue.

Carts aren't, however, compatible with real links golf. They trample the fine fescue grasses and compromise the bump-and-run nature of the greens and their bumpy surrounds.

From the start, Ladenburg had put together a team to build and operate the course.

"I didn't want them at odds, but working together," he said.

Heritage Links would build it, and KemperSports, which operates Bandon Dunes Golf Resort, would manage it. Even with the successes at Bandon, they feared a walking-only proviso at Chambers Bay would cut revenue by a third.

Not only would cart revenue be missing, but so would golfers who simply couldn't – or wouldn't – walk the several miles and elevation changes it takes to negotiate the dunes of Chambers Bay.

"I'll never forget it," said Bruce Charlton, the lead architect for Robert Trent Jones II. "There is this big meeting and John announces, 'We'll call the course Chambers Bay, we'll open in 2007 and we'll be walking.' Just like that."

So the course wasn't to be a resort. It wasn't going to be called "The lovely links of Puget Sound," or anything like that. The money the county was putting up wasn't going to be spent on a spa or even a clubhouse. The course wasn't going to be bastardized with bentgrass greens or concrete cart paths.

Nothing was going to get in the way of the dream. ✳

Top: In the lead-up to Chambers Bay's opening, Ladenburg continued his campaign of bringing USGA officials to the site. Here he confers with David Fay, who for 21 years was the executive director of the USGA and was an active champion of bringing the U.S. Open to public golf courses. When Fay retired at the end of 2010, Mike Davis, with whom Ladenburg had already established a relationship, replaced him.

Bottom: Among those attending Opening Day on June 23, 2007 were (left to right) Tony Tipton, the county's project manager; Mark Luthman, who was then the regional director of operations for KemperSports; Joe Scorcio, the deputy public works director for Pierce County during the building of Chambers Bay; Ladenburg; Bruce Charlton, the chief design officer for Robert Trent Jones II; and Jay Blasi, one of the on-site project architects for Jones.

THE VISION

51

Is there any other course with such
views for those not actually playing it?

CHAPTER 3

The Community

THE QUESTION WAS ALWAYS WHAT TO DO WITH THE SPENT LAND next to Puget Sound, land that was uncommonly ugly and beautiful at the same time, land that somehow deserved to be as requited as it had been ravaged.

Pierce County purchased the property for $43 million in 1992, both as expansion land for its water treatment plant and for its long-range potential as waterfront recreational property.

In all, there were 900 acres. But how and when to develop it?

The cost of building the Chambers Bay golf course – $24 million – seemed reckless to many. Why spend that kind of taxpayer money to build a course only rich folks can afford?

Point well taken.

Then again, in the mid-1970s Seattle spent $67 million (or, $275 million in 2007 dollars, the year Chambers Bay opened) to build the Kingdome – its early home for professional football and baseball – only to have it blown up 24 years later as being obsolete.

Key Arena's massive – and expensive – renovation lasted 10 years before the NBA turned its back on Seattle, citing an inferior facility.

Far from becoming obsolete, Chambers Bay would only get better with time. A hundred years from now, players would still be trying to figure out the humps and bumps of the great old course.

OPENED IN 1976, THE PUBLICLY-FUNDED KINGDOME, *located in the south end of downtown Seattle, cost $275 million to build (in 2007 dollars, the year Chambers Bay opened), and was the original home of the NFL's Seattle Seahawks and MLB's Seattle Mariners. The domed stadium's construction company said it was "built to last for a thousand years" – and it was demolished in 2000 for being obsolete, exactly 24 years after it opened. In 2016, the taxpayers of Seattle and King County pay off the bonds used to build the Kingdome, 40 years after it opened and 16 years after it was erased from the Seattle skyline.*

And those playing it might be trying to relive some great historic moment from the U.S. Open. Perhaps, as there is at Royal Birkdale in England, there will one day be a plaque in the rough right off the 18th fairway telling us about the 4-iron Rory McIlroy, or another legendary player, hit in the final round at Chambers Bay to win the Open.

Surely there would be other Opens here to create a growing archive of accomplishments and their memories. Surely after the 2015 Open, playing Chambers Bay would be on the bucket list of every golfer. The course would have a past to go with its potential. A course improved, not depleted, by the fits of nature.

And once the construction debt was paid off – in 2046 – the course could be a continuing source of revenue for the county as well as be the magnet for tourism and economic development that former County Executive John Ladenburg foresaw.

Because as much as it is world-class golf, Chambers Bay is also a local gathering place, a park, a trail, a vista, a destination. It allows access not only to the course, but to a beach and a grassy amphitheater.

It is in some ways already iconic. Indeed, the cement holding pens that remain along the 18th fairway are relics of Tacoma's mighty industrial past, a "Northwest Stonehenge." The Lone Fir that stands beside the 16th tee box is immediately recognizable in any photo of the course.

If it becomes "America's St. Andrews," then the same kind of foresight that put aside land in the middle of Manhattan for Central Park, or the best parts of the American wilderness for national parks, will have occurred at Chambers Bay, in creating a distinctly Puget Sound place to be and play, its uses as diverse as family picnics along the beach and the world's most demanding golf tournament, America's national championship.

From that perspective, the county's involvement will have made sense on a global level with the ongoing publicity for the area. And it will also have made sense on a local level with the preservation of the property and its varied uses by the public.

Community's Beacon

The Lone Fir at Chambers Bay is an ironic icon for a golf course that is pure links, and without trees.

But against the backdrop of Puget Sound and the snow-dappled Olympic Mountains, the Lone Fir is as sentinel as the lighthouses at Turnberry in Scotland and Hilton Head Island's Harbour Town in South Carolina.

There were those who campaigned for its removal to help authenticate the links course being fashioned out of a sand and gravel mine, and certainly many nearby trash trees were removed.

The final attempt (hopefully) to take it down came in early 2008, just months after the announcement that the 2015 U.S. Open had been awarded to the fledgling course.

In the early morning of April 30, work crews found a pile of empty beer cans near the tree and a gaping wound in the trunk near the base, the result of several swings of an axe sometime during the night.

Called to the scene of the crime, the first arborist on site deemed the fir a goner.

But David Weineke, Chambers Bay's superintendent at the time, refused to lose the great tree. He contacted Neal Wolbert, the president of Wolbert's Plant Essentials in nearby Olympia. And Wolbert contacted an arborist, Rob Lloyd.

Together they went to work, strengthening the tree against possible storms with a couple of metal straps and then doctoring the gash with an epoxy resin laid over the tree's own sap.

They also set out to improve the tree's root structure and, in fact, the fir looks better today than it did before the attack. Still, Wolbert and Lloyd worry about the tree, that it is not getting the continued attention it needs.

It remains revered, and famous, especially on the eve of the U.S. Open and the loss during an ice storm in early 2014 of the famed Eisenhower Tree on the left side of the 17th fairway at Augusta National.

Upper right: The wounded Lone Fir in 2008, shortly after the attack.

Lower right: By 2011 the tree had rebounded, becoming fuller and healthier than it was before the attack.

The Lone Fir continues to be a backdrop for wedding ceremonies, as well as a home for bald eagles, and as a point of reference for golfers and for walkers on the trail that traverses the course.

"To my surprise," said Matt Allen, the course's general manager, "we had literally hundreds of calls from people offering help, including replacement trees. People didn't love this tree because they were tree-huggers – they truly love this place and have a sense of ownership of it."

Chambers Bay is as open, and as vulnerable, to the public as any course in the U.S., and common sense and community spirit, not locked gates, will therefore be its guardians.

Ladenburg, who muscled the project through county government, understood from the beginning that Chambers Bay needed grassroots support, and that the public needed to be included, not excluded.

One of his early moves was to cut down trees along portions of the rim of the property to give the public a peek at its potential, allowing them to see not only the sand and sediment left by a century of excavation, but the beach beyond the railroad tracks, and the islands and mountains beyond that.

So that they could feel included, that this was their land, their view.

Ladenburg talked not about the property's isolation – there were groups that wanted to leave it undeveloped for what would amount to wilderness trails – but its integration into the county's recreational future.

The course architects lining up to compete for the project were told, unconditionally, that any golf course built would be dissected by a public walking trail, and that any scheme for the area would include use of the beach and the lands north and south of the course for public gatherings.

The trail has been a magnificent addition.

It provides momentary glimpses of play and of the beauty of the course without the players being aware they are being watched.

The trail begins as a grand promenade along Grandview Drive overlooking the course, with long-range views of every hole, a perhaps unprecedented perspective.

Is there any other course with such views for those not actually playing it? People flock to see the Magnolia Lane entrance at Augusta National – site of the Masters – because they aren't allowed to see anything else.

Pebble Beach has access along a toll road but the great seaside holes can't really be seen or appreciated by the everyday walker and jogger.

Heading north, the trail at Chambers Bay leaves the course as it traverses its way to the beach through a forested area that is home to bald eagles. It rejoins the golf course along the railroad tracks, where it meanders through and then climbs steeply past the amphitheater and back toward the restaurant and small clubhouse.

It is a little more than three miles around and often the site of fun runs. There are always more people walking the trail than playing golf, upwards of 5,000 a day during nice weather. Even in the dead of winter the walkers, cyclists and joggers persevere.

An important off-shoot in the development of the area is the bridge across the railroad tracks which has opened up two miles of sandy beach that, even before Washington statehood, had been private property.

So let's talk of how the same kind of foresight that put aside land in the middle of Manhattan for Central Park, or the best parts of the American wilderness for national parks, occurred at Chambers Bay in creating a distinctly Puget Sound place to be and play.

On a sun-splashed day it is difficult to think of Chambers Bay the way the county traditionally has, land for the expansion of its wastewater treatment plant which sits just south of the golf course at Chambers Creek.

The money spent on the land – around $40 million, all told – came from the wastewater district, not the county.

"If the money for the property had to have come from the county's general fund," said Joe Scorcio, then the deputy county public works director, "it never would have happened. The utility district had to grow. It had a necessity, and it had the money."

Scorcio had nurtured the project since the early 1990s. He was involved in the purchase of the land, had headed a committee to pick the architects, and oversaw the initial recreational development of the entire property.

"It is so improbable that it all happened," he said from his office overlooking nearly all the 900 acres. "In the beginning, when we purchased the land, it had nothing to do with golf. We had to support the wastewater utility. In the end, we needed something that would not only use reclaimed water, but bio-solids we produced for fertilizer."

So it was that the utility needed a compatible neighbor that not only allowed public access but might provide some revenue.

There wasn't an option to leave the land wild, as some suggested.

"We would have ended up with 600 acres of Scotch broom and alders," Scorcio said. "Nothing else would grow. The land needed to be reclaimed."

While the utility had the money to buy the original property and pay to expand its use, it could not pay for anything that didn't have to do with wastewater.

The county was in search of a revenue producer. A golf course was mentioned from the beginning, but not until Ladenburg came along in 2000 as county executive was there any thought of a "super" course.

"There's no question," Scorcio said, "that John spent his political will to get it done. He found a way to win every 4-3 vote."

Above: As his dream course neared completion, Ladenburg continued to preach about the property's value as a recreational asset for golfers and non-golfers.

Right: Joe Scorcio, the longtime deputy county public works director who dealt with the nuts-and-bolts of the entire 930 acres of Chambers Creek Properties including the wastewater treatment plant, was one of the first to understand the compatibility of a golf course with the overall needs of the county, both from a utilitarian and a recreational standpoint.

THE COMMUNITY

"We never wanted to keep the public separated from the golfers,"
Scorcio said. "We always felt they were compatible."

While the trail was popular from the day it opened – by walkers, joggers, cyclists, bird watchers – it surprised many how popular the restaurant in the makeshift clubhouse would be.

As Ladenburg would say to anyone who would listen, how much west-facing view property for restaurants is there in and near Tacoma?

Almost immediately, the restaurant at the top of the hill was embraced by the outside public. It began producing revenue the county needed. It was used more by diners than golfers.

Soon there was a championship high school cross-country meet on the Central Meadow, where Intel had held its annual corporate picnic for a crowd of 3,000. There was an opening-day concert. The Central Meadow will prove a wonderful staging opportunity for the U.S. Open.

In late 2011, the local community built a play structure next to the North Meadow and within sight of the 13th hole.

"We never wanted to keep the public separated from the golfers," Scorcio said. "We always felt they were compatible."

People stop on the trail near the ninth tee to watch what will become one of the most exhilarating shots in golf: a 100-foot drop-off-the-cliff tee shot to a green-bunker complex that looks like a piece of sculpted art. They often stop and applaud good shots hit by the casual golfer.

It seems a joy for Ladenburg and Scorcio and others that Chambers Bay is not some hidden Mecca for golf, but a true public place.

St. Andrews, the home of golf, is owned and operated by a public land trust. It promises its seven courses will forever remain open to the public, and that on

THE COMMUNITY

Sundays the Old Course will be closed, not only to give it a rest but to allow the public to walk its hallowed grounds. Throughout the week there are historical tours arranged to guide people to certain parts of the Old Course. The mid-week tours are 50 minutes, and there is a three-hour tour on Sundays.

Like Chambers Bay, St. Andrews doesn't give golf away. Its green fees – $240 for the Old Course in the high season – are higher than those at Chambers Bay. Locals, just as they do in Pierce County, enjoy considerably lower rates in the winter when the tourists are gone and the course really struts its stuff – its fairways so firm players don't need to improve their lies, let alone clean their shoes.

Scorcio believes that Chambers Bay is not about today or tomorrow, but about 50 years from now.

"Because the public utility isn't going anywhere – it will be here as long as people flush their toilets – we could think differently," he said. "Everyone wants Chambers Bay to turn a profit as a golf course – and it is, but this isn't about how many rounds it gets next week or next year. Or about getting it ready to sell to a private developer."

He paused and looked out over the vista above the fescued layout.

"This is about forever." ✳

Public Domain

Golf has been played in the small college town of St. Andrews, Scotland, for more than six centuries. The town re-acquired its one golf course in 1894 following the passing of the first Links Act by Parliament, safeguarding public access to the course for locals and visitors alike. There are now seven golf courses in St. Andrews, and the St. Andrews Links Trust, a charitable organization, was formed in 1974 to manage the publicly-owned courses. The Old Course, in keeping with a centuries-old tradition, is closed on Sundays to golfers, leaving it to walkers, picnickers and hikers to enjoy its seaside setting.

Chambers Bay has a three-mile long trail that meanders around and through its grounds and fairways, open every day to walkers and strollers. The trail is used by over 60,000 visitors each year.

Also on the grounds – Chambers Creek Properties – are two miles of shoreline along Puget Sound, accessible by a pedestrian bridge; a total of six miles of trails; North Meadow and Central Meadow together make up 28 acres, on which numerous community festivals, outdoor cinemas, fun runs and concerts are held; two off-leash pet areas; Chambers Creek Labyrinth; several multi-use playfields; and Chambers Creek Canyon, an urban forest with hiking trails.

Imagine the land as it was then, mountains
of sand hanging precipitously over the
edge of the waters of Puget Sound.

CHAPTER 4

The History

THE EVOLUTION OF CHAMBERS BAY BEGAN SLOWLY – literally at grinding, glacial speeds – as the Ice Age scoured out Puget Sound and left, in certain places, soaring hills of sand and gravel.

And in others, clay and mud.

While a bottomless pit of sand was to be found at one end of what is now the Chambers Creek Properties, at the other end – across the creek – there was good old Northwest goo, the result mainly of a glacial runoff from Mount Rainier, 65 miles to the southeast.

Blessed geologically, the north side of the creek was to have as fine a sand and gravel deposit as there was in the world.

Winding its way down from British Columbia, the glacier that carved out Puget Sound pushed up – and ground up – rocky materials, the result being what would become known as "Steilacoom Grade" sand and gravel.

"It was truly a remarkable deposit," said Scott Nicholson, the foreman at the plant when the property was sold to Pierce County. "The materials here traveled thousands of miles – some from British Columbia – and were extremely hard and clean, just the very best there was. Truly a remarkable event."

Imagine the land as it was then, mountains of sand – at about the height of what is now Grandview Drive, the boulevard that overlooks the property – hanging precipitously over the edge of the waters of Puget Sound, bulk-headed finally in the early 1900s by the building of what are now BNSF railroad tracks.

According to Pierce County historians, while a blip in time compared to the Ice Age and what followed, the quarry's human history dates back centuries to at least the Steilacoom Tribe, described as a small group of Salish-speaking Native Americans who lived along the east shore of Puget Sound in what is now the town of Steilacoom. There is evidence of an ancient summer fishing village near the edges of Chambers Creek.

The first European settlers didn't show up until the early 1800s, and then principally in the form of the Hudson's Bay Company and the Puget Sound Agricultural Company.

Fort Steilacoom, built just south of Chambers Creek, was the PSAC headquarters and commercial trading settlement until it became a U.S. Army outpost formed to keep the peace following establishment of the Canada-U.S. boundary in 1846.

There can be no doubt about the importance of Fort Steilacoom, both to the area and the future of the country. Beginning with its construction in 1849 until its closure in 1868, the fort served as what its chroniclers called "a beacon of American power and promise, promoting the migration of settlers to Washington and securing American interests in the region."

The name Chambers came from the legacy of Thomas Chambers, a judge and one of the area's first settlers.

For a few years in the early 1900s, William Kennedy owned a small strip of land alongside Chambers Creek, across from the paper mill. A fisherman, Kennedy lived on the land, plying the waters alongside tribal fishermen during the salmon runs. The strip of land became known as Kennedy's Camp, and was later used as a summer vacation spot.

Thomas Chambers

In a story in the Steilacoom Historical Museum Quarterly, Chambers was called the "Father of Western Washington Industry."

Born in Utenards, Ireland in 1795, Chambers was an ordained Presbyterian minister. He married Latitia Delzel, a cousin of former U.S. President Andrew Jackson, and they moved to the U.S. as Chambers became an overseer at Jackson's tobacco and cotton plantation in Tennessee.

Along with the nation's largest-producing sand and gravel mine, the property has also been the site of numerous businesses and industries, including multiple lumber companies, a paper mill, a railroad center, a bus barn, a regional wastewater treatment plant, a preservation and recreational area and, today, a golf course.

This photo from 1926 shows the West Tacoma Paper Mill along the banks where Garrison Creek emptied into Chambers Bay. Built in 1919, the mill manufactured book paper from pulp, and continued operation under various owners until closing its doors for good on December 31, 2000. It was the last paper production mill on the West Coast.

The mine was made up of several pits that merged and split over the years, and some companies even operated on the property simultaneously.

For over a century, seven different companies mined roughly 250 million tons of gravel from the site. It is estimated that 80 percent of the gravel and sand was transported by barges that could haul from 2,000 to 10,000 tons of material at once. Larger barges replaced an average of 250 trucks per trip, which cut highway traffic and provided a more direct route to destination ports.

In photo at lower left, today's Central Meadow of the Chambers Creek Properties is located in the middle, and the sorting bins near the top of the photo are now concrete remnants that still stand along the south side of the 18th fairway.

Chambers, his wife and eight children headed west in a wagon train to Oregon's Willamette Valley in 1845. Two years later they moved north and settled on disputed land near Fort Steilacoom. According to author Linda Perez, officials of the Hudson's Bay Company visited Chambers near the creek that would later bear his name and made their case.

"Chambers replied by resting a rifle on his fence and made it quite clear he was here to stay," wrote Perez.

The Hudson's Bay Company never bothered him again.

The Oregon Treaty of 1846 established the 49th parallel as the border between the U.S. and Canada and determined the future states of Washington and Oregon.

In 1850, Chambers began to build his business empire by opening the first three-story grist mill near the mouth of what is now Chambers Creek. Machinery was shipped from San Francisco and a thriving industry began.

Over the last 200 years, the entire Chambers Creek Properties area has been used as a location for a paper mill, multiple lumber companies, a railroad center, a county gravel mine, a bus barn, a regional wastewater treatment plant, a preservation and recreational area and, today, a golf course.

Who could have imagined that the predominant use of the land would end up being a golf course – and not just any golf course, but a celebrated sporting venue that would end up attracting global attention?

While much can be made of Chambers Bay's strategic and historic location on the edges of Puget Sound, the essence of its importance was in its soils. Both then and now.

Chambers Bay would never have been selected to host a U.S. Open if the course was anything less than a genuine links, built on sand, shaped with sand – firm and fast like the great, ancient courses of the United Kingdom.

As usual, need dictated use. In the early 1890s, the federal government selected Pacific Bridge Company to construct Fort Casey, Fort Worden and Fort Flagler, strategic military locations guarding the entrance to Puget Sound.

Each installation was to be surrounded with concrete bunkers, and this created a huge demand for sand and gravel.

THE MINING BEGINS

Mining on the property began in earnest in the early 1890s when the Pacific Bridge Company, which had been mining gravel on the site since 1859, was selected by the federal government to construct Fort Worden, Fort Flagler and Fort Casey, strategic military locations at the north end of Puget Sound where it met the Strait of Juan de Fuca and fed out to the Pacific Ocean. These three forts were made mostly of concrete, with materials drawn from the mine, and were completed in 1905.

The three forts became obsolete almost as soon as they were built. The invention of the airplane made them vulnerable to air attack, and the development of battleships transformed the stationary military defenses of the 19th century into the more mobile systems of the 20th century.

Long since abandoned, the forts are now part of the state park system, vacation destinations for hikers and campers. They are listed in the National Register of Historic Places in the United States, which is administered by the National Park Service.

Fort Worden (top) is located at the north end of the town of Port Townsend; Fort Flagler (middle) is on the north end of Marrowstone Island, along Port Townsend Bay; and Fort Casey (bottom) is on the west side of Whidbey Island, a short ferry ride from Port Townsend.

Pacific Bridge was one of the two fledgling gravel mines operating where the Chambers Bay golf course now lies. There began a procession of barges leaving the site and heading up the Sound to the military bases.

According to Pierce County, "Subsequent owners over the next century enjoyed the rich gravel deposits found at the Properties. By 1992, Lone Star Northwest had merged all the gravel mining on the Properties into the single largest producer of sand and gravel in the nation."

How large-scale was it? In 1992 – the year Pierce County purchased the property – Lone Star moved 3.2 million cubic yards of sand and gravel off the site, the most in recorded American history. Eighty percent of the materials were transported from the site by barge.

"Ninety percent of the Seattle skyline was built with materials from our operation," said Nicholson, who came to the site in the early 1980s as a callow 19-year-old.

"I stopped by the union hall looking for a job," he said. "They said I could shovel gravel for a couple of weeks at Steilacoom. I didn't know that was the beginning of a 30-year career."

Nicholson is the aggregates director for Glacier Northwest, which is now part of the CalPortland conglomerate. As foreman at Chambers Creek, Nicholson supervised 30 to 40 workers and watched as many as five or six barges a day leave the property.

The company continued to mine the site seriously until 2000, when Pierce County officials began shutting down the operation and making plans for the reclamation. The north side of the site – up near what is now the 13th fairway – was

The raw materials from the mine were used to build the interstate highways that crisscross the Puget Sound region, and most of the Seattle skyline was built with "Steilacoom Grade" gravel from the mine.

Opposite page: In the tunnel underneath the sorting bins, the sand and gravel was washed and sorted before being loaded onto the waiting barges. The massive remnants of these sorting bins now line the south side of the 18th fairway, and entrances to the tunnel can still be seen at their base.

Although Pierce County purchased the property in 1992, Glacier Northwest continued to operate the mine until late 2003. The once-famous and seemingly bottomless gravel pit, being mined out, closed forever in December 2003.

Symbols of the land's century of sand and gravel production remain in the remnants of huge holding bins along what is now the 18th hole.

still heavy with sand, but most of the gravel had been mined and shipped. In the final year of mining – 2003 – only 150,000 cubic yards left the site, a fraction of the kind of mining that had gone on just a few years earlier.

Pierce County retained the mining permits long after Lone Star was gone and that helped considerably in the freedom to move sand around to build the golf course. The irony is that today, to keep the golf course in tip-top shape, there needs to be consistent applications of sand to the fairways and the greens and some of it will have to be shipped in.

Although more than a million cubic yards were moved during the building of the golf course, not everything was bulldozed and forgotten. Symbols of the land's century of sand and gravel production remain in the remnants of huge holding bins along what is now the 18th hole.

Walkers interested in the history of Chambers Bay can peek from the public trail into the tunnels that run under the bins, tunnels that housed the rumbling conveyor belts that moved the materials down to the shore to waiting barges.

There also remains – across the railroad tracks – an 11,000-square-foot abandoned dock, a creosoted temple to another time when sand and timber were so plentiful in the dawn of the region's industry that there was little concern they might someday be gone.

The dock will be torn down when the "Bridge to the Beach" is finished, when there is money to connect it to a modern moorage site, when boats will bring people to the area instead of hauling away its indigenous soils. ✳

"There are so few places in the world that offer sandy soils and a maritime climate. Our charge was to use the site wisely and create golf art."

CHAPTER 5

The Architects

IN 1951, ROBERT TRENT JONES SR. CHANGED THE FACE OF GOLF.

He had to, as new equipment – primarily steel shafts for the clubs – was making mincemeat of traditional layouts.

The elder Jones turned Oakland Hills Country Club northwest of Detroit, that year's U.S. Open site, into what eventual winner, Ben Hogan, called a monster. Jones had pinched in fairways with bunkers at 250 yards and surrounded elevated greens with sand, requiring from top players what his son calls "the aerial game," the kind Jack Nicklaus would conquer and later design.

Hogan shot one of the only two rounds under par during the week at Oakland Hills. The monster roared.

Now, more than 50 years later, the son, Robert Trent Jones Jr., has changed golf again, this time with wide, fast fairways that require precision more than power, a course than can test the mighty and please the proletariat, a sustainable course that requires less water and fertilizer. A course that, as he put it, is fun and playable, yet is a strict test of skills.

One that secured a U.S. Open, and in the process took us back to another era in golf.

"When I got the call to come to the USGA press conference to announce the Open was coming to Chambers Bay, they asked me if I had a plane ticket to get there," Jones said. "I told them I didn't need one – I'd get there on cloud nine."

> "Bobby could see a course that could host a U.S. Open when all I could see was brush. To me, that's the genius of it all."

Robert Trent Jones Jr. and his team stood amid the property's scrubby terrain in the early going, near what would become the teeing ground for the 16th hole.

It didn't escape Bobby, as he's known to his friends, that, until this moment, the most recently-built course in America to get the U.S. Open – Hazeltine National in Minnesota – was designed by his father.

Robert Trent Jones Jr. is among other things a poet. It was his job to give the layout at Chambers Bay imagination and variety, for the routing to have harmony and rhythm, for the course to be an examination of a player's skills, but not relentlessly difficult.

"I walked the property with Bobby when you couldn't see 10 feet in front of you," said Pierson Clair, the CEO of Tacoma candy-making giant Brown & Haley and a longtime friend. "Bobby could see a course that could host a U.S. Open when all I could see was brush. To me, that's the genius of it all."

Like so many others, the Request for Proposal for a golf course near Tacoma, Wash. came without fanfare across Bruce Charlton's desk. It asked for the design of a publicly-owned, 27-hole layout on the shores of Puget Sound.

"We like government assignments, public-spirited projects that advance the game," said Charlton, Bobby's partner and the president and chief design officer of the golf design firm of Robert Trent Jones II.

But Charlton was soon beyond everyday altruism, or the excitement that comes from building just *any* golf course.

"Hold on, time out," he shouted to his two young associates, Jay Blasi and Mike Gorman. "Take a look at this."

It didn't take them long to understand the potential of reclaiming a sand and gravel mine that had for years been itself a reservoir of materials that built great courses, and that now, in a silent but persistent way, wanted to become one itself.

To test-drive the drawings, project architects hit hundreds of golf balls (these on what would become the 18th fairway) in what golf course architects and their crew call a "Dirt Open" – get the clubs out and find out what works and what doesn't work, because what you draw in your office 500 miles away sometimes doesn't make any sense when you are on the property itself.

One That Got Away

Walking by himself in the large gallery following the semifinal matches of the 2010 U.S. Amateur being held at Chambers Bay was John Harbottle III.

A native of Tacoma, one of the finest of men in the region's golf community and a scion of Northwest golf royalty with both his parents being members of the Pacific Northwest Golf Hall of Fame (with his mother, Pat, having won the 1950 U.S. Girls' Junior and the 1955 U.S. Women's Amateur), Harbottle was an award-winning golf course architect who had desperately wanted the job of designing Chambers Bay, a course to be built literally in his backyard, and indeed had been one of the five finalists in the county's selection process for an architect.

After a few holes watching the matches, he was approached and asked what he thought of the course. "There are 17 world-class holes here," he said with a smile.

Harbottle passed away suddenly in 2012 at the age of 53.

"We raced for Google Earth," Charlton said, "to understand the land's relationship to Puget Sound, but even then – those were Google Earth's early years – we didn't fully understand the drama of the location."

Nearly 60 design firms replied to the original request. Pierce County winnowed the list to five, which besides RTJ II included one led by Phil Mickelson and another by local favorite John Harbottle. Bob Cupp and Michael Hurdzan completed the five finalists.

"I just thought Bobby, more than the others, believed in our dream to get a U.S. Open," Pierce County Executive John Ladenburg said. "I also knew that he had the contacts with the USGA that could help us get it done."

Ladenburg sought the opinions of others in selecting the architect, but would make the decision himself. It proved a difficult one, as he ultimately chose Jones over Tacoma's Harbottle, a personal friend, who had already proven his skill as a course designer with his previous work.

Before he passed away in 2012 at the age of 53, Harbottle, watching the 2010 U.S. Amateur, graciously said of Ladenburg's decision, "You have to understand that I wanted this job in the worst way and didn't always agree with what the Jones folks did. But having said that, Chambers Bay is a wonderful golf course. They have 17 world-class holes."

Harbottle wasn't a fan of the par-5 eighth hole that stretches high along the rim of the course and is bunker-less but not toothless. He loved the others, however.

Within a week of Ladenburg's decision, the RTJ II crew was on site. In fact, Pierce County officials had to, after a while, usher them off the grounds of what was still considered a working mine.

"The site," Blasi said, "cried for a great links course."

Not all the would-be architects saw it that way. There were designs that left trees and highlighted water features. RTJ II complied with the request for a 27-hole design, but then, with great passion, offered one of 18 holes. Plan B.

"I said to our team as we went into the interview that we might be shooting ourselves in the foot," Charlton said, "but it was my feeling that if we were going down we'd go down with our guns blazing."

At the end of their session with Pierce County officials, Blasi handed out bag tags for the 2030 U.S. Open at Chambers Creek, as the future course was initially referred to.

Surely the act was audacious. But who could have imagined that it would undersell the timeline of the project by 15 years?

As the story goes, Blasi was attending the PGA Championship at New York's Oak Hill Country Club in 2003 when he happened to stand next to a bag-tag maker. The wheels were turning.

"He told me he could do a minimum of 50," said Blasi, who now values them as a collector would.

He admits that any sane projection for Chambers Bay as an Open site would have been 2030 or later. A modern course hadn't been selected for decades. Even if the course were perfect, it was reasonable to expect 10 to 15 years of play as an audition, then another decade before it actually happened.

But the stars were aligned – along with the land, soils and commitment from Pierce County – to build a great course, and a chance for Robert Trent Jones Jr. to create a legacy that would have made his late, famous father proud.

Bobby's younger brother, Rees, had become, as their father had in the 1950s and '60s, a noted "Open Doctor," working to remodel some of golf's most venerable venues – Baltusrol, The Country Club, Bethpage Black and Congressional, among others.

Bobby, who says his best work is still ahead of him, knew Chambers Bay was a chance for greatness. He wanted to draw "golf art," as he calls it, across the sandy face of this gravel pit along the shore of Puget Sound; be the conductor of a symphony that included not only his other designers, but especially the shapers, the men who move dirt, and in this case, sand.

"They are the quiet laborers in the vineyard who make the wine, while the architects plant the grapes," said Jones, poetic, as usual, in pinpointing the work of shapers Doug Ingram and Ed Taano. The latter has been with Jones for years, and would later craft the subtle changes to Chambers Bay, sketched and overseen by Jones, that the USGA wanted in preparation for the 2015 U.S. Open.

"The views are spectacular, and although some holes are striking, like No. 10 and No. 15, this is not a pretty course," Jones said of Chambers Bay, which steadfastly has no flower beds or water features. "The course is gritty, reflective of the work done here. Chambers Bay has inherent beauty because every hole has strong golfing character with many playing options, with un-level teeing grounds, wide treeless fairways and contoured greens. The features of the course are complemented by the extraordinary natural beauty of Puget Sound and the Olympic Mountains."

It became all about making the course look and play as if it had been carved by the winds of a thousand years.

Jones called his friend Clair, the candy company operator. Could he find a boat

Surely the act was audacious. But who could have imagined that it would undersell the timeline of the project by 15 years?

At the conclusion of the Jones team's presentation to Pierce County officials in bidding for the contract to design the course, the architects presented them with bag tags for a 2030 U.S. Open at "Chambers Creek" with the county logo in the center.

in which they could float off-shore? They motored quietly into the Sound so Jones could not only see the property from that perspective, but could feel the winds. He wanted the sand dunes that would define the course to look as if they had been made over time, not with modern earth-moving equipment.

He wanted the course to have what he called "rhythm and harmony," to ebb and flow, a routing that would have demanding holes followed by relenting holes, bogeys followed by birdies.

As an apprentice at RTJ II, it was Blasi's first design effort. Newly hired by Jones and Charlton, he was 25 when he first stepped onto the property, a kid playing literally in a massive sand box that would be transformed into an acclaimed $24 million project.

"I couldn't have dreamed of a better opportunity," said Blasi, who knew and helped shape the heart and soul of every fairway and green, habitually hitting golf balls at them during the construction phase to see potential avenues of ruin and reward.

The Jones team sold itself to Pierce County, and then sold the county on a links course replete with fine fescue grasses, a combination that, while common in the United Kingdom, was embraced in America primarily at Bandon Dunes Golf Resort on the southern Oregon coast.

While the makings of a links course were there from the get-go, the county threw potential architects a curve when it required that every proposal include 40-plus acres of catch-basins to facilitate the dispersal of wastewater from the nearby treatment plant.

Most of the architects put the areas within the confines of their proposed courses. The Jones team posted the 40 acres outside the course and decided, ultimately, to save only one tree, a single evergreen behind the 15th green.

Later, the county realized that because of improved technology, the ponds were no longer required, and so the Jones plan became prophetic as well as successful.

"I think we had John's (Ladenburg) ear when we talked about 18 holes instead of 27," Charlton said. "We told him that if he did 27 holes a lot of them would run parallel. We said, 'John, if you really want to catch the world's eye, then 18 holes is the way to go.'"

By this time, Ladenburg had selected KemperSports, which had done an amazing job putting and keeping Bandon Dunes on the map, as the management company for Chambers Bay.

Ladenburg (left) had selected the Robert Trent Jones II architectural firm to create a dream course because he felt that Jones (right), more than the other candidates for the job, had the experience and the connections to land a major championship for the fledgling course. The two men, both driven, knew what the goal was, and worked in unison toward it.

EVOLUTION OF AN ICON

The short par-3 15th is probably the most recognizable hole on the course. With the Lone Fir behind the green, silhouetted against Puget Sound, the hole is immediately identifiable in any photograph.

The first sketch of the green complex (upper left) was drawn by Jones in March 2005. Rather than a design, this was an early conceptual imagining, a quick study, to get a sense of how the hole would flow from left to right.

A year later, in February 2006, Jones put pencil to paper for another sketch of the green (upper right). This second, and final, drawing is the closest to the end design – in completing the green complex, Jones worked on it on site with shaper Ed Taano.

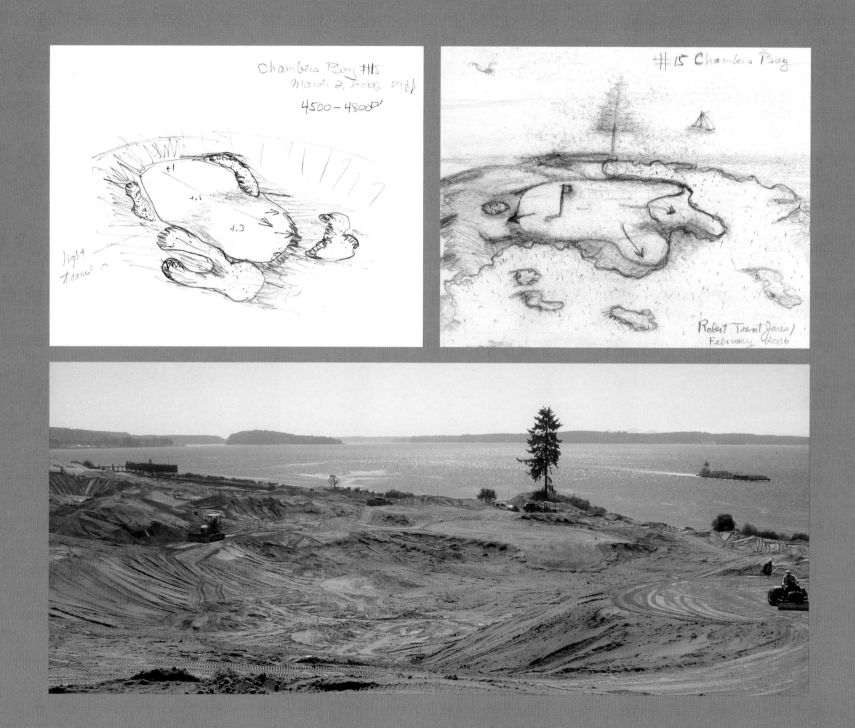

When Pierce County officials sent out the Request for Proposal to golf course architects who might be interested in designing a golf course for them on a vacant piece of property along the shores of Puget Sound, they were very clear about one thing – they wanted three nines, 27 holes, and the golf course had to accommodate 43 acres of water bodies for sewage effluent storage.

When the firm of Robert Trent Jones II presented their case to the county in bidding for the job of designing what would be known as Chambers Bay, they gave them what they had asked for – a fully integrated plan consisting of 27 full-length holes, a "Master Plan" (left) that wound its way over the nearly 300 acres.

And then they took a chance by also giving them something else – an alternative plan (right) that called for a muscular 18 holes with its own routing over a majority of the property, along with an executive nine holes, a practice course that had a maximum length of 2,430 yards and located at the south end of the property.

It was this alternative plan that sold the Pierce County decision makers on the Jones team. By this time, the county had already begun to formalize their goal of landing a major championship, and when Bruce Charlton passionately presented this alternative plan to them during the final architectural interview, they realized the Jones team understood what the ultimate goal was and, more importantly, how to get there.

Later, after they had won the contract, Charlton would further massage the routing of the 18 holes, moving the clubhouse eastward onto the top of the hill, and would eventually discard the notion of the executive nine, replacing it with a larger practice facility.

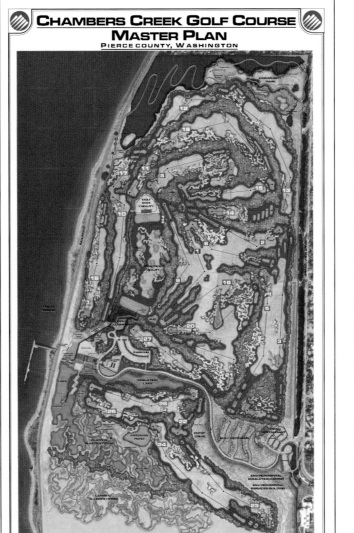

The calloused hands of the artists

Talk about a big job.

After finishing Paul Fireman's Liberty National across the water from Manhattan, Heritage Links, a division of Lexicon Inc., the golf course construction firm based in Houston, Tex., had little time to regroup before taking on the biggest challenge of its expanding portfolio.

When all was said and done on the shores of Puget Sound, with 50 men, 25 major scrapers and countless off-road dump trucks, Heritage Links moved more than a million cubic yards of sand and gravel to build Chambers Bay, carefully making reality out of Robert Trent Jones Jr.'s dreams and drawings.

They artfully plowed a fairway through a sand dune to make the most contrived hole – the revered No. 10 – into the most organic looking. You think you're at Ballybunion in Ireland.

"That was the biggest challenge for Heritage," said Tony Tipton, the project manager for Pierce County. "To create a natural looking golf course when the land they started with was so scarred and deformed from mining activities."

And Heritage Links, which would work with Jones later in renovating the Prince course at Princeville on the island of Kauai, did more than just build a golf course. They constructed the temporary clubhouse on the hill, as well as the starter shack by the first tee. They also built one of the property's most important – and most used – features, the walking trail around and through the course.

Jon O'Donnell, the division president of Heritage, estimated that of the $16 million his firm spent to build the project, $11 million went to building the golf course while the rest was spent on the path, the clubhouse, the parking lot and the general infrastructure needed to get to and from the course.

While working with sand is an architect's dream, Heritage Links found so much sand that it at times battled keeping its equipment from sinking.

The final touches in making the course look natural were to take the smooth dunes and run dozer tracks up them. Some of the tracks can still be seen today.

"We're pretty proud of what we did there," O'Donnell said. "It's a great golf course and was built with a true team effort." Heritage Links received the 2008 Builder Excellence Award for its work on Chambers Bay.

It was obvious that the massive scope of the job narrowed the field bidding to build Chambers Bay, and Heritage also had the advantage of having worked with Jones on other projects. "I think we had Bobby's seal of approval early on, and that helped," O'Donnell says.

Chambers Bay holds a special place for O'Donnell, whose son, Joshua, was born on Feb. 7, 2008 in Houston, the same day that the USGA announced, in Houston, the 2010 U.S. Amateur and the 2015 U.S. Open would be played at Chambers Bay.

O'Donnell has a framed copy of his son's birth certificate hanging on the wall next to a copy of the press release from the USGA.

"He'll be with me at the Open," said O'Donnell. "That's for sure."

"All that sand. I'm not sure if they knew what they had. Sand is like gold to an architect. I spent the next couple of hours running up and down the dunes to see what could be seen next."

The downhill, dogleg-left par-4 14th hole (seen here during construction and shortly after completion) is appropriately named "Cape Fear." The fairway skirts what amounts to a seven-acre waste area on the left side, a remnant of the more than one million cubic yards of sand that was moved to mold the course.

Josh Lesnik, the initial general manager of Bandon Dunes and later president of KemperSports, had also lobbied Ladenburg hard on the plans, adamantly telling him to just build the best 18 holes he can.

Later, when asked about Chambers Bay's chances of succeeding, Lesnik said, "If Jones builds a great golf course it will be met with great success. It's no more complicated than that."

For Jones himself, the depleted site was a great and beckoning canvas.

"Where great land meets great water there can be great golf," he said. "There are so few places in the world that offer sandy soils and a maritime climate. Our charge was to use the site wisely and create golf art."

The world is full of links-like courses. Courses with lots of bunkers and few trees, with lumpy greens and fairways. Great courses in the Nebraska Sandhills. Great courses on the East Coast like Shinnecock Hills.

But few of them replicate Scotland and Ireland the way Bandon Dunes and now Chambers Bay do because the fine fescue grasses can't thrive at many other American venues.

Bandon Dunes, with its first course opening in 1999, had paved the way in the use of fescue grasses which, while yielding fairways that are as fast and firm as greens, were vulnerable to too much cold and too much play.

At Bandon, the courses were built without cart paths and players were forced to walk and carry their clubs, or use a caddie to do the latter.

While it authenticated the site, a decision to prohibit cart usage – and cart paths – had implications beyond design and aesthetics. Serious money would be lost in the form of cart revenue and the loss of those who might play but wouldn't – or couldn't – walk the 18 holes.

The Jones team agonized. They saw at least six greens that could not be built to their links limits if cart paths were used. An example was No. 10, the glorious par-4 up through the excavated dunes.

Charlton and Blasi remember the meeting. And the decision. It might not have been popular at the time, but it was pivotal. The decision was necessary because fescue turf has a limited capacity to handle traffic, and divots recover slowly.

Ladenburg, whose vision of creating a course capable of hosting the U.S. Open was on the verge of being realized, was simply not going to let cart revenue get in the way.

The architectural drawing of the green complex for the 17th hole.

By the spring of 2013, most of the renovations being performed on the course had been completed. In March of that year, during the annual summit meeting of the Golf Alliance of Washington being held at Chambers Bay, Bruce Charlton, the chief design officer for Robert Trent Jones II, gave a tour of the course to the meeting's attendees, detailing the reasoning behind the renovations.

The meeting took place in early 2006 in downtown Tacoma. "I'll never forget John saying, finally, that it will be called Chambers Bay and we will walk it in 2007," Blasi said.

So the questions became what to do with the property, how much sand and gravel to move, whether to have the clubhouse near the water or on the hill, how to at all times exploit the views – how to make the course exceptional for both the casual and accomplished player.

As they combed the ragged edges of the property, Charlton was struck by the possibilities, not just on a local or national level, but for a course that could draw worldwide attention and respect.

"This," he said to Blasi, "could be absolutely world-class."

The materials were not only already there but the permits to treat it as a mine gave the RTJ II boys almost unlimited range and creativity in developing the property. At this point their sand box knew no limits.

Early on, the first hole to declare itself was No. 12, the short uphill par-4 that had been a roadway for gravel removal.

Then what to do south of the now-famous Lone Fir along the railroad tracks?

The ultimate tack was to take what would become the 16th and 17th holes down to almost track level, and to do so they tipped the land, and the fairways, toward the water.

To get to No. 11 they cut through the dunes for No. 10, which looks like the most organic hole on the course but simply isn't.

"We were so excited," Charlton said. "I remember being at a Christmas party at Bobby's house (in the San Francisco Bay Area) and talking to Ron Read, who was then the western regional director of the USGA, and telling him to keep an eye on what we were doing."

What they were doing was moving more than a million cubic yards of sand and gravel. They lowered what would become the 13th hole some 25 feet and used the highest grade of sand on the property to provide capping for much of the rest of the course.

They were able to make the fairways so wide you couldn't miss them, but at the same time could be hazards for a skilled player trying to make birdie, requiring tee shots to specific areas.

THE ARCHITECTS

As the Jones team surveyed the property during the process of preparing their proposal to Pierce County in bidding for the contract to design Chambers Bay, this was the first hole to declare itself. It had been a road used by Glacier Northwest, the sand and gravel company who owned the property prior to the county buying it in 1992, to move sand from the rich deposits north of the property.

In the initial plans that Jones presented to the county, this was to be the third hole on the course's routing. After the Jones team had won the contract, and the county leaned more and more toward building an 18-hole layout rather than their initial thought of a course with 27 holes, the Jones team altered the routing, with this hole becoming what it is today – the 12th hole, a short, drivable, uphill par-4, with a massive multi-leveled green complex hidden in a hollow.

Love of Course

Three weeks prior to the 2010 U.S. Amateur, Jay Blasi, the on-site project architect for Robert Trent Jones II in creating Chambers Bay, married Amy Spittle in a small ceremony overlooking the 15th hole and Puget Sound. Amy works for KemperSports, the course's management company, and the two met during the opening phases of the course.

Whereas Tom Doak did minimal moving of soils to create Pacific Dunes, and while at Whistling Straits, Pete Dye was trying to turn a Midwest lakeside pasture into Ireland, the work at Chambers Bay, while perhaps more contrived, ended up looking more natural because of the sand, because of the sea.

On his first visit to the site, Blasi couldn't believe his eyes.

"All that sand," he said. "I'm not sure if they knew what they had. Sand is like gold to an architect. I spent the next couple of hours running up and down the dunes to see what could be seen next. Believe me, it was tons and tons of fun."

During the three weeks following their first visit to the site, in what amounted to an "all hands on deck" approach to one of the largest proposals they'd ever prepared, Charlton handled the permit and code details while Blasi and Gorman worked 20-hour days to finish their plan. Or plans, as it turned out.

"I've learned," Charlton said, "that if a government asks you for a 27-hole layout, then you'd better give it to them. But we decided to show them what 18 holes without the wetlands for wastewater would look like."

It was, especially with Ladenburg, a winner.

"A true links course doesn't have internal water bodies," Blasi said. "We had the weather for a true links course, but to complete the deal – you don't go 95 percent of the way – we needed fescue grasses and no cart paths."

The go-ahead was for 18 holes. Ponds were precluded by changes in wastewater technology. Finally, Ladenburg directed that there would be no cart paths.

At one point during construction, the principals met in New Jersey at famed Pine Valley, where Jones is a member. In developing Chambers Bay, Jones said Pine Valley's vast sandy waste areas had more influence on his design than any other course.

It was here, too, that Ladenburg assured the USGA in the person of Mike Davis that anything and everything would be done to host an Open. Davis was, in other words, given carte blanche – he need only ask for what he requires to make it happen, and it shall be given by the county.

It was happening.

"There is a Chambers Bay because of John Ladenburg," said Pierson Clair, "and there is a U.S. Open because of Bob Jones." ✳

Opposite page: Looking back down the fairway of the par-4 sixth hole.

Beyond the fiscal realities of the worldwide economy, Chambers Bay faced cultural differences as well, the fact that it didn't – and never would – look and feel like other American courses, especially other Northwest courses.

CHAPTER 6

The Recession

IT WASN'T THE BEST OF TIMES TO OPEN A GOLF COURSE, not in 2007, a year ahead of the worst economic news since 1929.

As with the opening of a new and ballyhooed restaurant, there was an initial rush to play Chambers Bay. During its first year, the course attracted nearly 40,000 players, enough to meet payroll, so to speak, as well as make payments on the daunting debt amassed in building the course.

Pricing was pivotal to the success of the course. Too high and it would turn away locals. Too low and it might bring more play than the course's fine fescue grasses could survive.

Tony Tipton, the project manager for Pierce County, said back then that the goal was to attract 32,000 players a year at an average green fee of $100 per round. That, he said, would produce enough revenue to cover operating costs and pay down the large and looming debt.

At first, Chambers Bay withstood the economic downturn – the Great Recession – because of the surprise announcement by the USGA that both the U.S. Amateur and U.S. Open would soon be staged there.

It was like a white puff of smoke from the Vatican. Chambers Bay had been anointed. It would be only the third municipal course in the country to hold the Open – Bethpage Black and Torrey Pines the others – and be the first on any course in the Pacific Northwest.

The number of rounds played held steady through 2008, but began to dip the following year. They remained above the national average as the golf industry as a whole took a dive, but failed to generate enough money to make the annual debt payment.

Driving Wheel

In the back of the van that shuttles players from the rim overlooking Chambers Bay to the first tee is a map of the world.

Into this map are stuck red pins that show the far-flung residences of those who have come to play the muni, from distant lands ranging from Siberia to New Guinea, from Austria to Australia.

Without question, Chambers Bay will be on the bucket list for most avid golfers, as it is one of only a handful of U.S. Open sites that allow public access.

So they come from far and near. Nearly 10 percent of the course's website traffic is from international visitors. In 2013, 30 percent of the play at Chambers Bay came from local Pierce County residents, and of the remaining 70 percent, a quarter of those came from outside the state of Washington.

During the peak season of most years the golf course employs 150 staff, and the U.S. Open will have a projected economic impact of $144 million on the area.

Pierce County was forced to step in.

A couple of factors were in play. For one, the condition of the greens did not justify summertime, out-of-county $175 green fees.

And, too, projections that rounds would average $100 didn't pan out. For half the year, when the weather was truly British Isle-like, most of the rounds were generated locally and there was little interest among Pierce and King County users to pay repeatedly more than $100 to play in the rain.

As is often the case, those nearest the project were most critical. While national magazines fell all over themselves lauding the course, provincial naysayers concluded the greens weren't good enough for a national championship.

Abetting the negative buzz was that the failure to secure private funding for a clubhouse fueled hearsay that the USGA would pull the Open from Chambers Bay.

However, the USGA kept pouring money into the project, making changes – many of them minor – to almost every hole and showing no signs the Open faced a change in venue and Chambers Bay an ignominious defeat.

Mike Davis, who would become executive director of the USGA in 2011 and who first saw Chambers Bay while in his role as the association's senior director of rules and competitions, loved the course at first sight, and loved it still.

"So many possibilities," said the man who had changed the Open from a staid and strenuous test of narrow fairways and ankle-high rough to an imaginative test of drivable par-4s and unreachable par-5s.

During the buildup to the Open, the problem wasn't the USGA or the lack of love of the course by cognoscenti of links golf.

Rather, the problem came from the failure of the greens to grow and the publicity that came from continued conversations about the course losing money.

Midway through 2012, *The Seattle Times* reported losses for Chambers Bay of "more than $4 million from 2009 to 2011."

The reality was that during only one of those years did the course itself lose money on its operating budget. The money that was lost was that pledged to make payments on the debt.

So Pierce County had to shoulder the load.

And, despite the persistent rumors, there was no reason to think the USGA was alarmed by the reality that no private developer had been found to build a clubhouse.

"We can build a temporary clubhouse for the U.S. Open," said Reginald Jones, the USGA's senior director of U.S. Open Championships. "We built what we needed at Torrey Pines (in 2008)."

While the failure to repay the debt caused great consternation among some citizens, Pierce County officials said in a *Tacoma News Tribune* story that the course was moving toward breaking even in 2014. The number of rounds played in 2010 increased 19 percent as KemperSports officials scrambled to induce play by offering annual passes to local players. Restaurant revenue in the small makeshift clubhouse also had increased.

While there was concern that sewer district taxes were being used to pay the debt, there was also the reality that the sewer district would have had to maintain the gnarly 300 acres of property even if a course had not been built.

Brian Ziegler, head of the Public Works and Utilities District, said the sewer utility was meeting a legal requirement to pay back the course for maintenance and would continue to do so.

Pat McCarthy, who replaced John Ladenburg in 2008 as county executive, chose to look beyond early losses. She talked about not one U.S. Open at Chambers Bay, but many of them. She also talked about the recreational benefits of the course and its surrounding trails and beach.

McCarthy told the *Tacoma News Tribune*, "I applaud the fact that we took that piece of moonscape and turned it into the potential for a revenue generator, and more importantly, a beautiful public space for the public to enjoy."

And, clearly, the worm was turning at Chambers Bay. As the major renovations for the Open – and the disruptions caused by it – came to an end in 2013 and unusually good weather persisted through the spring and summer of that year, operating revenue was up more than $1 million from the year before. There was no need to dip further into the county funds to service the debt. With nearly 40,000 rounds played, Chambers Bay was close to realizing the initial plan for self-sufficiency.

There was also an increasing hum about the Open and an appreciation for better turf conditions, as well as strong interest in annual and seasonal memberships and their accompanying preferred green fees.

The only problem was that with the Open on the horizon, maintenance costs were beyond what had been originally forecast.

Still, the numbers were encouraging. Through most of 2013, rounds played were up 15 percent, the highest since 2008, and revenue was up 24 percent. In addition, sales for Open merchandise inside the small pro shop had increased almost 75 percent compared to the year before, and rounds played by out-of-state golfers also began a steady increase in the two years prior to the Open.

Caddies to the Core

Maybe it is because the population is growing older, but the time-honored use of a caddie is growing steadily at Chambers Bay.

In 2013 the course did 30 percent more caddied rounds than the previous year. In July and August of 2013 there were 3,000 bags toted over the dunes of the fledgling U.S. Open venue.

"There are a growing number of players who have no desire to carry or push their clubs," said Brian Haines, the course's manager of caddie services since its opening in 2007. "And they enjoy the true links experience that comes with having a caddie."

The out-of-town, summertime, bucket-list players use more caddies than do the locals. Some want prompting on every shot, while others want nothing but someone to carry their bags.

There is a core of 30 or so caddies that has been with Haines since the course opened, and overall there are more than 90 in the caddie pool. Some have done more than 2,000 rounds, and Haines expects a few to be on the bag during the U.S. Open.

And as was proved at the 2010 U.S. Amateur, local caddies are worth their weight on a course where knowledge is king and the use of a rangefinder can be only mildly helpful.

In the long days of summer, a caddie might carry two bags for two rounds. Chambers Bay is a rigorous walk with several elevation changes, and to do it twice with bulky bags is a challenge.

The caddies are high school kids looking to earn an Evans Caddie Scholarship, college students, college graduates who haven't found work, retired guys looking for something to do. And everything in between. The eldest caddie is 79.

Many of the caddie core are vagabonds, as Haines calls them, heading south in the winter to find work – to Palm Springs or Arizona, even Florida.

"I don't care if they have caddie experience as much as they have golf experience," said Haines, who retired from the auto industry and wanted to be around golf, with no idea he'd end up with a full-time job.

Blushing from the recent announcement that it would host the 2010 U.S. Amateur and the 2015 U.S. Open, yet reeling from the onset of the economic recession, Chambers Bay in its early years was the site of a few events, initial attempts by the fledgling course to establish a name for itself among the game's elite players.

In 2007 and 2008, PGA Tour player Ryan Moore, who grew up in nearby Puyallup, Wash., hosted a skins match in which he brought a few of his tour friends out to raise money for local charities.

Playing in the event both years was Bubba Watson (here teeing off the par-3 15th hole), while other members of the foursome in 2007 included PGA Tour players Michael Putnam (left, in light blue sweater), who grew up in University Place just a few miles from Chambers Bay; and Aaron Baddeley (in blue sweatshirt, with arms folded).

Moore would later serve as the honorary chairman of the 2010 U.S. Amateur, a championship he won in 2004.

In September of 2013, at the USGA's request, the turf was completely removed from the greens on No. 10 and No. 13 and both were reseeded, an unheard-of move with the Open less than two years away, but also a vote of confidence for the new agronomy direction at the course.

Beyond the fiscal realities of the worldwide economy, Chambers Bay faced cultural differences, the fact that it didn't – and never would – look and feel like other American courses, especially other Northwest courses, where in the summertime grasses are lush, greens smooth and in some cases lightning quick, the beneficiary of long sunny days and nearly unlimited water for irrigation.

The job at Chambers Bay was about changing perceptions as much as it was about growing grass.

Why fescue, the fragile grass that thrives only in certain climates and soil conditions around the world?

It was the same reason the course wouldn't have golf carts, even though they were proven moneymakers and made the layout accessible to so many more players.

"We wanted an authentic experience," said Matt Allen, the general manager at Chambers Bay, who had cut his teeth on the Bandon Dunes experience and knew the appeal of playing a links course – pure, real, unadulterated golf.

There were other reasons to bring a bit of the British Isles to the Puget Sound area that is by definition a "green" area politically and climatically.

With fine fescue grasses you could use much less fertilizer. And less water. And you didn't need to mow as often. You could spend less money and less energy and have surfaces that were faster and firmer than anything seen north of Bandon Dunes and west of Ireland.

Green was a bit of a misnomer for the course that in tournament-ready conditions was far from green. Butterscotch might better describe a links course in waiting.

Early on, the look was met with a critical eye. The course and its hopes of hosting the U.S. Open looked as if they were drying up.

Could the USGA admit it made a mistake awarding the Open to Chambers Bay before its time? Could the scruffy course in the Northwest really follow Merion and Pinehurst, hallowed venues, in the Open lineup?

The USGA was out on a limb here. Chambers Bay would defy the laws

of American golf, which had become a game played in the air, with accurate measurements of distances gleaned not only from course markers but now, in a new age, from personal GPS technology.

At Chambers, distances wouldn't matter, not when the fairways were more linoleum than lush, when they might – like they are at the Old Course at St. Andrews – be as fast as the greens. Or faster.

There are plenty of links-style courses that don't deal with the so-called fine fescue grasses, even great American courses like Shinnecock Hills. Whistling Straits, the modern links design along Lake Michigan by Pete Dye, has fescue fairways, yes, but also bentgrass greens.

There were only a few places in the world where the soil and climate conditions would allow for fescue grasses to flourish, as they do in the British Isles and in parts of New Zealand.

Was the area around Puget Sound one of them?

Once the Robert Trent Jones II team was on site, there was never any talk about trying to build a links course at Chambers Bay without using fescue grasses on the greens as well as the fairways.

And it was pretty obvious that the USGA would have far less interest in the site as a future Open venue without the fescue experience.

Bandon Dunes had done the experimental work, its seaside courses wildly popular even though they didn't look or feel like traditional American layouts.

But University Place was almost 500 miles north of Bandon's southern Oregon location. Later measurements would determine that the ground temperatures averaged much cooler in winter along Puget Sound.

For the most part, the interest in fine fescues throughout much of the American golf scene was cosmetic – tall, wispy grasses that framed holes.

There is no question that Chambers Bay has struggled with its bold attempt to create a links course with fescue grasses – struggled with keeping the indigenous Poa annua grasses out, and the fragile fescue alive, especially in well-traveled areas.

The architects never envisioned sawdust paths between holes, but it became evident that the fescue couldn't handle the wear and tear in critical areas – fescue isn't particularly hardy, susceptible to deterioration from too many people walking on it.

But what fescue does is give the course wall-to-wall sameness. During the subsequent renovation of the seventh hole, a temporary green was mowed out of the fairway and it became as good as any green on the course.

Perhaps trying to get a new course ready for a national championship – the 2010 U.S. Amateur – had come too early, or been too much. USGA officials wanted the superintendent to discontinue the eradication of moss as the course prepped for the championship, and by the time the championship was over, the moss had infiltrated much of the greens and the decision was made to kill it in the fall of 2010.

The problem was that once the moss was dead, the onset of winter's wet and cold weather compromised growing new grass to flesh out the greens where the moss had been. There was some improvement in the spring, but the greens were simply unable to grow enough to deal with the wear and tear of play.

"They hadn't hardened," said Eric Johnson, who was lured away in 2012 from the Old Macdonald course at Bandon Dunes to fix the problems at Chambers Bay.

It isn't that the greens had to have the usual Open speed of 12 or 13 on the Stimpmeter. The rumbling, rambling greens designed by Jones would be all Open contestants could want even at 11 on the Stimpmeter. Moreover, for most of the year and most of the players, a Stimp reading of nine or 10 would produce plenty of fun and 3-putt greens.

But the USGA had lingering concerns. Certainly the course could be firm and fast for the U.S. Amateur in August – and it was blazingly fast for the 2010 championship at Chambers Bay – but what about the U.S. Open in mid-June?

June is a transitional month in the Northwest, not yet summer, still spring, often cool and wet to the chagrin of the natives.

What if it rained much of May and on into June? Could the density of the rough be controlled, would the fairways and especially the turf surrounding the greens be firm enough?

"If we get two weeks of dry weather before the Open the course will be very firm," said Larry Gilhuly, the northwest director of the USGA Green Section, whose job it is, from his nearby Gig Harbor home, to keep track of the progress at Chambers Bay. "Even if we have rain, it will be firm enough."

But Gilhuly understands the problems.

When he first heard that Chambers Bay would have fescue greens, and not bentgrass, he said to himself, "Well, they better make the greens big enough. And have room for a lot of selections for hole locations."

Gilhuly, in grass-speak, uses the term "negative wear tolerance."

"They can't have too much play in the winter. It could wipe out the greens," he said.

In fact, it almost did. But into the summer of 2012, conditions began to improve.

"The caddie master told me for the first time he wasn't getting complaints about green speeds," Gilhuly said. "They upped the fertilizer and used more consistent mowing and rolling patterns. The big greens were good, the smaller ones, like No. 6 and No. 10, were still experiencing wear difficulties as players exited the green in one area."

After the Amateur, the USGA went to work. Davis and other USGA officials swept in for a meeting with Chambers Bay staff, as well as Robert Trent Jones Jr. and Bruce Charlton from the design team.

Changes were made both to add additional pin placements, as well as give the players a proper reward for a well-struck shot.

But even as the greens improved, there remained the challenge, a conundrum, really. Chambers Bay needed enough play to produce revenue to pay off the debt, but not too much play as to wear the place out. ✳

Everyone in golf at its loftiest levels was watching. Not only was the fledgling course trying to show itself capable of doing justice to our national amateur championship, everyone also knew this would be the trial run for the U.S. Open.

CHAPTER 7

The First Test

WHEN AMERICA'S OLDEST GOLF CHAMPIONSHIP – THE U.S. AMATEUR – was played in 2010 on one of its newest courses – three-year-old Chambers Bay – who could know what might happen?

With a Slope rating of only 146 from its championship tees, few forced carries and in some places 100-yard-wide fairways, would Chambers Bay be tough enough? Or, with its lumpy greens and rock-hard surfaces, would it be too tough?

Everyone in golf at its loftiest levels was watching. For not only was the fledgling course trying to show itself capable of doing justice to our national amateur championship, everyone also knew this would be the trial run for the U.S. Open scheduled to be held there five years later.

When it was over, when a field of the finest amateur golfers on the planet had been whittled to one – U.S. Amateur champion Peter Uihlein – the verdict was clear. Chambers Bay had what it took to be a great U.S. Open site.

"The cream rose to the top here because Chambers Bay tests all those things," said Tom O'Toole, at the time the chairman of the Championship Committee for the USGA. "It tests shot-making capabilities, rewards well-executed shots and penalizes poorly executed shots." O'Toole would become USGA president for the two years leading up to the 2015 U.S. Open.

The week wasn't without travail, including some pretty scary moments as the course appeared early on to be screaming for water, turning a caramel, almost butterscotch color.

In August 2010, Peter Uihlein was the No. 1-ranked amateur in the world. On August 29, the day of the final match, he turned 21 years old. Teeing off the par-4 first hole in the afternoon round of the 36-hole match, Uihlein (above) held a 2-up lead over David Chung. Six weeks prior to the U.S. Amateur, Uihlein had won the Sahalee Players Championship, held that year at The Home Course, just 10 miles south of Chambers Bay.

But, in the end, it delivered the way the USGA hoped it would as the first Amateur to be played on a public course.

First of all, the U.S. Amateur, which is usually played in front of family and friends, was extremely well attended at Chambers Bay. It even made money for local organizers.

For the 36-hole championship match, held on the final day, more than 5,000 spectators followed the final twosome, Uihlein, the Oklahoma State star, and David Chung, the Stanford junior. They were appropriately the No. 1- and No. 4-ranked amateurs in the world. The cream had, indeed, risen to the top.

Celebrating his 21st birthday on the day of the final match, Uihlein, scion of Wally Uihlein, the CEO of golf manufacturing giant Acushnet, won the Amateur on the 16th hole, the 34th of the match, defeating Chung 4 and 2 for the title in its 110th version.

Local golf journalist Paul Ramsdell wrote, "As the two came together to shake hands and Chung conceded defeat, Puget Sound loomed beautifully in the background and the dunes above the hole were filled with most of the 5,250 spectators who followed the final match."

The spectator count for the week was 33,700, exceeding the optimistic goal of 30,000 projected by organizers. An official from the host committee said ticket sales and corporate sponsorships more than covered the nearly $1 million Chambers Bay had to raise to pay for hosting the championship.

In the final analysis, Ramsdell wrote, the championship was decided on the far northwestern corner of the 7,461-yard, par-71 layout as Chung came up short after attempting one of his patented back-nine comebacks.

"When we were 4-up with that back nine left, I knew David was going to do something, and he did," Uihlein said of Chung, who had rallied from a three-hole deficit the day before in his semifinal match against defending champion Byeong-Hun An.

Chung cut the four-hole deficit down to two, when Uihlein made a bogey out of a fairway bunker on No. 10, and Chung holed a 25-footer for birdie on No. 11.

"I thought, 'Hey, if I make a couple of putts here I could get something started,'" Chung said.

"The cream rose to the top here because Chambers Bay tests all those things."

For the final match, the USGA's Mike Davis had moved the tee markers on the 16th hole forward a hundred yards from the day before, so that the par-4 was played at just 289 yards long. The hand-held scoreboard tells the story of what would turn out to be the last hole of the match – that Uihlein was 3-up with three holes to play. He had hit first off this tee, conservatively laying up short of the green. Chung, running out of holes and needing to make something happen, swung away, and the result can be clearly seen by Uihlein (in lower-right corner of photo on the left) pointing left to alert the forecaddies up ahead.

Chung made two attempts to punch out of the fescue onto the green. When he was unable to do so, he conceded the hole and the match to Uihlein.

THE FIRST TEST

And just when it appeared Chung could draw to within 1-down as Uihlein pulled his drive into a waste area left of the 522-yard, par-4, 14th hole, the birthday boy escaped trouble with a shot that stopped 20 feet from the hole, from where he knocked in a birdie putt for a 3-up advantage.

The end came perhaps as Mike Davis, who set the course up for the championship, hoped it might, on the 16th hole, alongside the railroad tracks and the banks of Puget Sound.

Surprisingly, Davis completely altered the challenge of this hole for the final match by moving the tees forward 100 yards, taking the hole from 389 yards to 289. He was, in a sense, daring the one behind in the match to attempt to save himself by driving the green, and the one ahead to be careful, but not too careful.

Uihlein, standing on the tee with a 3-up lead with three to play, played conservatively and well, putting his hybrid tee shot just short of the green. Chung hit driver and ended up in the deep rough left of the hole, and after a couple of attempts at escaping the swing-strangling fescue, he conceded the hole, match and championship to Uihlein.

"You know," Uihlein said a year later, "I knew Chambers Bay was a long course and a tough walk, but what I didn't know was how great the green complexes were. In setting up the course, Davis put creativity back into golf. He forces you to look at a hole from the green backwards. You have to know your options. You have to evaluate and then execute."

To start the week, Chambers Bay shared the two qualifying rounds with the nearby Home Course, home to the Pacific Northwest and Washington State golf associations, a links-style course with great views of Puget Sound and Mount Rainier that had opened the same month as Chambers Bay in 2007.

It was on The Home Course that Uihlein, just six weeks prior to the 2010 U.S. Amateur, won the prestigious Sahalee Players Championship by seven strokes. The competition had been moved from Sahalee Country Club that summer because that club was hosting the U.S. Senior Open.

LOCAL BOY MAKES GOOD

John Bodenhamer served as the CEO and executive director of both the Pacific Northwest Golf Association and Washington State Golf Association from 1991 until 2011, and when the two associations purchased and opened The Home Course in 2007, he became the CEO of that golf facility as well.

He was instrumental in the success of The Home Course's participation in the 2010 U.S. Amateur as the companion course, and shortly after Mike Davis became the new executive director of the USGA in early 2011, Davis called on Bodenhamer to be part of his new senior management team at the USGA.

Within a year after the 2010 U.S. Amateur, Bodenhamer was named the senior managing director of rules, competitions and equipment standards for the USGA.

In the photo above, Bodenhamer (left) accepts a host-club gift from Jim Hyler, who was the president of the USGA at the time, during the ceremony following the conclusion of the 2010 U.S. Amateur.

Home and Home

On June 29, 2007, The Home Course opened to the public, just six days after Chambers Bay opened. Co-owned and operated by the Pacific Northwest Golf Association and the Washington State Golf Association, both of which serve as the regional arm of the United States Golf Association, The Home Course is located just 10 miles from Chambers Bay.

The Home Course served as the companion course for the 2010 U.S. Amateur, alternating with Chambers Bay during the first two days of stroke-play qualifying to narrow the field to the 64 competitors who then played the championship's matches at Chambers Bay.

The Home Course was also the site of the 2014 U.S. Women's Amateur Public Links Championship.

The year before, Uihlein won the Ping/*Golfweek* championship at Gold Mountain Golf Club in nearby Bremerton. Obviously, he was sold on the state of Washington.

Chambers Bay was most demanding for the two qualifying rounds. Almost too demanding, really.

Scores averaged an unheard-of 80 the second of the two rounds. Shots seldom stayed where they landed, but as it turned out the players didn't mind that much and the best of them advanced to match play.

"I've never played anything like this," said Brian Higgins of Bellingham, Mass. "How do you explain how firm the course is without dropping a ball on cement and watching it bounce."

Coming off the 18th green, Eric Steger of Noblesville, Ind. commented, "I wish the Open were here next year so I could see how the pros attack it. It is so unlike anything I've ever played, and so much fun. It's not the same shots you normally hit. You have to be creative, try things you've never tried. When you're trying to qualify for the U.S. Amateur, that isn't exactly comfortable, but it is awfully fun."

Nick Taylor, the University of Washington star and that year's most decorated collegiate golfer, said, "It is pretty insane, but also pretty fun. I've probably played it eight times before this month but it has never been like this. It is concrete with grass, but the same for everyone and a course that demands you be creative. It is an awesome match-play course. You have to hit two perfect shots to get a birdie putt. The reality is you can make a par and win a hole."

Scott Langley of St. Louis – the NCAA champion who advanced to the quarterfinals (and later to the PGA Tour) – talked about thinking his way around the course. "I had way too much fun in the practice rounds trying to figure things out by hitting balls off all the slopes around the greens. I was being a kid out there."

He mentioned stinging a 3-iron on the par-4 10th to keep the fairway bunkers out of play, and a short-iron on the par-3 third hole that missed the green by 10 yards but ended up near the hole.

"People probably thought I missed that shot," he said. "But it was where I knew I needed to hit it to stay on the green."

Links golf is supposed to be a random event, balls bouncing wherever. But, as Northwest Director of the USGA Green Section Larry Gilhuly observed later, sometimes too much is too much.

One official observed that of 90 balls that landed on the first green, only eight of them stayed there. On the seventh hole, balls often came bounding down the hill off the front of the green, sometimes rolling as far as 150 yards away.

Morgan Hoffmann hits his second shot on the par-5 18th hole during his quarterfinal match against Peter Uihlein. Both players would par the hole, giving Uihlein a 1-up victory in the match.

While officials couldn't add copious amounts of water during the qualifying rounds for fear of unfairly altering scoring, once match play began the water was flowing.

Davis admitted they'd let the course dry out too much, that it needed water and it got water. Things will probably be different for the Open, held in June, a transition month for the Northwest, sometimes summer, sometimes not.

As the week went on, Gilhuly said the course was just about perfect, the grass surrounding the greens as firm as the greens. He, too, admitted there were a few times when it was too firm, but added that it was all part of the learning process for the Open.

For the gallery, the viewing was spectacular, better perhaps than any previous U.S. Open venue and better than the Old Course at St. Andrews, where the use of double-greens forces fans to stay on the outer boundaries of what essentially is a flat piece of property.

At Chambers Bay, the manufactured dunes mean you can see almost everything from everywhere.

The winners of the U.S. Amateur were Uihlein, and the determined effort to return old-fashioned golf to fashion.

"I loved Chambers Bay," Uihlein said, looking back. "You've got to use the slopes and be creative. You've got to hit every shot with a certain spin and height. You've really got to control your ball."

Another winner was Chambers Bay superintendent, David Weineke, who was charged with making the course firm, but not too firm. "Weineke nailed this sucker," said Gilhuly.

It might also have proved Weineke's undoing, as in preparing the course for the championship a decision was made by the USGA not to eradicate the growth of moss on the greens. When Weineke did get to the eradication, it was too late. The greens suffered for almost two years trying to recover.

Weineke was replaced in 2012 as director of agronomy by Eric Johnson, who was lured away from Bandon Dunes. Johnson, along with superintendent Josh

To see if his hopes for Chambers Bay had been realized, the USGA's Mike Davis (left) watched the 2010 U.S. Amateur from every angle, already taking mental notes of the preparations that needed to be done for the 2015 U.S. Open.

THE FIRST TEST

So as the Amateur ended, and Uihlein's name had barely finished being engraved on the Havemeyer Trophy, there was talk about it coming back to Chambers Bay.

Left: Jim Hyler, president of the USGA in 2010-2011, conducted the ceremony on the 16th green along the shore overlooking Puget Sound following the conclusion of the final match.

Right: Course architect Robert Trent Jones Jr., who had spent the week at Chambers Bay watching the championship unfold, both congratulated and consoled runner-up David Chung after the final match. At the time, Chung was a sophomore at Stanford University in Palo Alto, Calif. Jones' office is near the campus, and in 2008 his design firm created a state-of-the-art short-game practice facility at Stanford University Golf Course. Later in 2010, Chung would ascend to be the No. 1-ranked amateur in the world.

Lewis, who himself had been lured away by Weineke from California's Pasatiempo Golf Club, began to turn the course around.

"I'm sure we won't get everything right in 2015 for the Open," Davis said. "But assuming that the championship will be back, we'll learn each time."

So while some are wondering why they ever picked this former gravel pit to host the U.S. Open, Davis is as much as saying that Chambers Bay could become part of an Open rota with other monster munis such as Bethpage Black and Torrey Pines South.

Davis said he never worried about the quality of the greens at Chambers Bay, or the eradication of Poa annua grasses from the greens and fairways. He said he did worry about the ability of Pierce County to spend the money to get the course ready — to finish it, as he put it, by attending to details such as edging bunkers and pulling out Scotch broom from the vast waste areas.

The flexibility of the course's design was on display at the Amateur, delighting Davis and most of the players. There can't be a more adjustable course in the world. It has six par-4s that can be made drivable and seven that can be stretched to 490 yards or longer.

As the winds shifted during the Amateur and whipped in from the southwest, Davis moved the tees back almost 100 yards on the much-photographed par-3 15th hole, to 246 yards, and then moved them up 100 yards on the par-4 16th, to a drivable 289. No one made much of it at the time, but the 11th hole, a downwind par-4, played 539 yards on one of the days, the longest par-4 in USGA championship history.

So, as the Amateur ended, and Uihlein's name had barely finished being engraved on the Havemeyer Trophy, there was talk about it coming back to Chambers Bay. Davis said the USGA decided a dozen years earlier to play the U.S. Amateur on U.S. Open sites. The players, he said, deserved no less than to be competing on these wonderful, historic layouts.

"If we get invited back to Chambers Bay (for the Amateur)," Davis said, "I can't imagine that we wouldn't look upon that as something very favorable."

In other words, yes. ✱

Pat McCarthy, who in 2009 had succeeded John Ladenburg as Pierce County executive, helped see his dream realized during the 2010 U.S. Amateur. Standing behind Pat is John Bodenhamer, who at the time was the CEO of The Home Course and the Washington State Golf Association and Pacific Northwest Golf Association, before being called by the USGA in 2011. Next to Bodenhamer is newly-crowned champion Peter Uihlein.

Brown is Beautiful

Shortly after Chambers Bay was awarded the 2010 U.S. Amateur and the 2015 U.S. Open, the course's architects brought up the idea of "fairways as hazard" in describing the intention in creating the firm and fast layout. In essence, they said, "Yes, we'll make the fairways 70 yards wide, but you will need to place your shots on the proper sides or portions of these rolling and thunderous expanses in order to score well."

Golf instructor Harvey Penick's famous advice to "Take dead aim" will not work on a browned-out links layout on which the fairways are rolling faster than the greens, as they were during the 2000 British Open at the Old Course in St. Andrews. Links golf is not linear – it is baroque and classical all at once. You don't want to aim at your target – you need to find out where your ball is going to end up after it stops rolling.

During hectic guided tours of the classic links of the United Kingdom, American tourist golfers wax nostalgic over the quaintly rugged and brown courses in the birthplace of the game – and then return stateside insisting their home courses be kept unrealistically and artificially green and lush, even in the heat of summer.

Links-inspired golf is the principle of working with nature, not against it. The uncommon common sense of links golf is beautifully simple – less waste of water resources; reduced usage of chemicals; naturally keeps at bay Poa annua, the scourge of superintendents everywhere; and requires skill and course management, rather than sheer power, to play, yet remains eminently playable and forgiving for the average golfer.

Oh, beautiful brown.

Brown is Brutal

The week before the 2010 U.S. Amateur, local player TJ Bordeaux, who had qualified to play in the championship, was out on Puget Sound in his uncle's boat, plying the waters between University Place and Steilacoom. Before long, Chambers Bay came into view. As they looked over the railroad tracks that separate the course from the water and saw the parched layout beyond, both men fell silent.

"We were shocked," Bordeaux recalls. "We couldn't believe how brown it looked. I had never seen it look anything like that before."

A week later, during the championship's first round of stroke-play qualifying over the dry and desiccated course, Bordeaux shot a 2-over par 73, a round which required enormous mental and physical effort.

"I know 73 doesn't sound good," he says. "But to start with three straight bogeys and then shoot 1-under for the remaining 15 holes, on that course, was pretty amazing. Andrew Putnam (another local player from University Place competing in the championship) told me afterward what a great round it was. It was such a grind. If you stopped concentrating for a single shot, you'd end up with a double-bogey."

Its enormous potential seemed to overcome its lack of tradition. And the simple fact was that the USGA wanted to take its premier championship where it had never been before.

CHAPTER 8

The Open

THE OPEN OF FIRSTS.

The first United States Open Championship played in the Pacific Northwest.

The first Open played on fine fescue grasses.

The first Open that could – if the USGA wanted – be played at more than 7,900 yards.

The first Open contested on a golf course built in the past 50 years.

The first Open on a course that could be more brown than green, or at least organizers hoped it might.

The first Open where one day a hole is played as a par-4, the next day as a par-5, and where the range in tee placements can be 100 yards or more on a single hole.

The first Open where thousands of spectators could watch the championship from a stationary position, sitting atop dunes, in grandstands, viewing multiple holes, like, well, the British Open.

The first Open televised by Fox Sports.

And the last Open where the anchored putting stroke is within the Rules of Golf.

This one is different, all right.

What a contrast, for example, with the 2013 U.S. Open at Merion, where the history is rich and venerable and the course sits on 125 acres, half the size of Chambers Bay.

But what Merion lacked in space, it more than made up for in tradition, with Bobby Jones clinching the Grand Slam there, and Ben Hogan striking the iconic pose as he nailed a 1-iron shot to the 18th green en route to winning his second of four Open titles.

The idea that Merion just wasn't long enough or tough enough or didn't have enough room to stage the Open didn't keep the USGA from embracing its past. And as it unfolded, Merion proved plenty tough enough even though fears of rain and soft greens materialized, with no players breaking par, and the champion, Justin Rose, winning with a score of 1-over.

If Merion was considered too old and too small, then Chambers Bay was certainly too young and too big. But its enormous potential seemed to overcome its lack of tradition. And the simple fact was that the USGA wanted to take its premier championship where it had never been before.

As the USGA was making the final changes to the golf course and began to envision how to handle 35,000 spectators a day, there were rumors that gridlock might hamstring Seattle and Tacoma, that the condition of the greens would send the Open to an alternate site – although there was none – and that the lack of a clubhouse meant the championship couldn't possibly be played there.

"Frankly," said Danny Sink, the USGA's on-site championship director, "it is better for us not to have a clubhouse. We didn't have one at Pebble Beach or Torrey Pines. Most of the clubhouses at established clubs are too small to work. We're better off using a tent."

In fact, a clubhouse on the hill near the restaurant – as John Ladenburg had envisioned in the beginning – might have been a liability for the Open, according to Sink, because it was simply too far from the starting and finishing holes.

Instead, the Open experience for spectators would start and end in an area called the Central Meadow, a large grassy area south of the 18th hole at Chambers Bay, an outdoor rotunda of sorts.

This is where the hundreds of buses would drop off spectators, where tickets are taken, shirts sold, newspaper stories written and, just to the north, on the 18th hole, the championship concluded, if not decided.

From his first visit to Chambers Bay in late 2010, Sink knew this would be a different Open from others he had organized.

"The first time I saw the course I couldn't see it," he said of a foggy, overcast December day. "But once it cleared I knew this was an amazing site. We've never had this kind of topography and elevation changes for an Open. You can see almost everywhere here."

Danny Sink (left), championship director of the 2015 U.S. Open, and John Ladenburg, on site prior to the championship.

Francis Ouimet's victory over English stalwarts Harry Vardon and Ted Ray at the 1913 U.S. Open is considered the birthplace of American golf. While John McDermott had become the first American-born champion (1911 and 1912), it was Ouimet, a 20-year-old amateur, who captured the hearts of the public, his victory bringing the Open to the people, to the general public, making golf an American game.

Ouimet (at top of photo, having been hoisted onto the crowd's shoulders) grew up across the street from The Country Club in Brookline, Mass., where he caddied during his youth. After qualifying for the 1913 Open, he employed the services of 10-year-old Eddie Lowery (middle, carrying clubs) and the two formed a special bond that remained intact long after the championship.

Ouimet went on to become one of the great ambassadors for the sport, winning two U.S. Amateurs and competing on six U.S. Walker Cup squads.

While the course was wide open and there was lots of adjacent space, the course presented its own problems.

Unlike the Olympic Club in San Francisco, where the main parking lot was at Candlestick Park, there was no obvious place to park 10,000 cars in Tacoma.

In the beginning, there were hopes that Chambers Bay's proximity to a major railroad line – the trains rumble past the 16th and 17th holes – and Puget Sound itself might allow for spectators to come to the course via rail and boat. And while the boat idea did not pan out, the BNSF agreed to allow a small platform be built for passengers to disembark near the Central Meadow, enabling patrons to get to the Open by rail from downtown Seattle, 30 minutes to the north.

The topography at Chambers Bay would prove a beauty and a beast for the Open, the dunes allowing wonderful viewing positions but also ensuring a tough go for those walking every hole.

The challenge would be moving gallery from near the Central Meadow to the northern reaches of the course – holes 12 and 13 – and up to the rim of the giant sand pit near the eighth green and the ninth tee.

"It's going to be like many of the British Opens, more of a stationary event where you've got these wonderful areas you can watch from and in some cases see multiple holes," said Mike Davis, executive director of the USGA.

While in the beginning there was talk of 75,000 spectators roaming the dunes at the Open, a closer look cut that number in half. Parking, no doubt, would limit the numbers. So would the dunes, especially around tees and greens where there simply isn't room for large galleries. There was also the danger of spectators slipping on the dunes, as they had during the 2010 U.S. Amateur.

Reg Jones, the USGA's senior director for the U.S. Open, said Chambers Bay would end up somewhere near the middle in terms of crowds, Merion in 2013 with 25,000 spectators per day the smallest, and Pinehurst in 2014 with 45,000 one of the largest.

Given the unprecedented interest in volunteering for the Open at Chambers Bay, as well as the rate in which corporate sponsorships were being sold, it was obvious that selling tickets was not the problem.

As spectacular as is the 100-foot fall from the original teeing ground on the downhill par-3 ninth hole, Mike Davis asked that an alternate tee be built that is actually below the green, to be used at the course set-up's discretion, which will require an uphill, into-the-wind 220-yard tee shot.

Showing the course's unheard-of flexibility, the 10th hole, seen here during the 2013 Washington State Amateur, could quickly be converted into a drivable par-4, or, from its normal tees, played simply as one of the world's most beautiful holes.

State Amateur's Dry Run

Two years before the 2015 U.S. Open at Chambers Bay, the golf world was focused on the 2013 Open at Merion.

But in the upper echelons of the golf industry, there was almost as much interest in that year's Washington State Amateur Championship, because it was held at Chambers Bay, and because it was held the same week as the Open and would serve as a not-so-dry run.

"Everyone kept asking me how Chambers would hold up if there was no wind or rain," said Scotty Crouthamel, the senior director of rules and competition for the Washington State Golf Association, which conducts the State Amateur. "And I'm still not sure."

Cameron Peck (shown above), who had won the 2008 U.S. Junior Amateur and is from nearby Olympia, had five eagles and seven birdies during the 2013 State Amateur, yet finished at even par, going wire-to-wire and winning by five strokes.

That's Chambers Bay. On the final day, with the wind whipping off the Sound, Peck shot 78 and only 22 players in the field broke 80.

For the U.S. Amateur in 2010, played in mid-August, the course was protected by its dried-out fairways and greens. "There is no way we will see those same conditions for the Open," Crouthamel said. "It won't be as firm and fast as it was that August."

June is a transitional weather month in the Pacific Northwest. Some Junes are wet, some aren't. Some are windy, some not.

For the State Amateur in 2013, there were a couple of dry, windless days, but on the final day a storm blew in from the southwest.

For the final round, Crouthamel used the new lower tee (the Mike Davis special) on No. 9, the par-3, and playing into a strong wind many competitors were hitting driver. Few hit the green.

In fact, the wind made another par-3, No. 17, the most difficult hole on the course relative to par. The tee shot was played from the lower tee next to the railroad tracks where it was fully exposed to the elements.

"On some holes with the wind blowing," Crouthamel said, "bogey is a good score."

Crouthamel said he favored No. 1 as a par-4, and No. 18 as a par-5, and realizes Davis might switch them around during the Open.

In September 2013, two greens (including No. 10, shown in top photo) were completely scalped and reseeded, the fescue being stressed by too much foot traffic on the greens' narrow entrances and exits.

Course shaper Ed Taano (above), who had done much of the original shaping of the course and had a hand in most of the subsequent major renovations, also increased the size of fairway bunkers on both sides of No. 5, pinching the landing area for the hole's tee shots.

"We could have sold 75,000 per day if we had wanted," said Jones. "But we wanted the best experience possible for those there."

And while it was important to take advantage of the site "outside the ropes" from an operational standpoint, it was decisions made on what would happen inside that would make Chambers Bay a fixture in the U.S. Open rota.

Or not.

On a cold day in January of 2011, Robert Trent Jones Jr. and Bruce Charlton, the architects, met at Chambers Bay with Davis and his USGA specialists from both inside and outside the ropes.

They walked the course and virtually took it apart, hole by hole, almost shot by shot. There was much to evaluate.

The fourth green, cut into the steep hillside bordering Grandview Drive, had already been made larger and slightly less severe for the 2010 U.S. Amateur.

When the course opened in 2007, the fourth hole – an uphill, sweep-to-the-right par-5 – became constant entertainment for those watching from the walking path above the hole. Shots played anything but perfectly could circle across the green and race for a sandy cliff right of the green. From that point, balls tumbled into the vast waste area below.

Watching shots coming back toward the green – some making it, most not – was almost as entertaining.

The Amateur, played on as firm conditions as there could possibly be, suggested similar changes be made to the greens at No. 1, No. 7 and No. 13.

During the Amateur, a USGA official charted approach shots to the massive first hole, a long par-4. The hole was meant to be approached from the high side, good shots landing short and right of the green and then spilling onto it.

Of 90 balls that reached the green during one stretch, only eight of them stayed on the green, most cascading down a steep hillside left of the green to finish 100 yards from the hole.

"We pushed to the edge," said Jones, "and occasionally we pushed too far."

In discussing the necessary renovations, it wasn't Davis versus Jones, although at times it could have been. They both showed great respect for one another.

After watching approach shots during the 2010 U.S. Amateur roll as much as 150 yards back down the fairway on the uphill par-4 seventh hole, its green was lowered and shifted to the right in 2012. In addition, to entice players to challenge the waste area right off the tee, a large hummock blocking the left approach was widened and increased in height.

"We wanted the course to utilize the characteristics that the architects had imagined and built," Davis said, "but sometimes it took some modifications to get those results."

Balls hit uphill to the seventh green – perhaps as demanding a par-4 as there is in golf – often came back off the green and down a steep grade, sometimes rolling as far as 150 yards from the green.

Davis was also concerned about the challenges Chambers Bay would offer if the weather turned benign. Its fairways were often five times as wide as those at a traditional U.S. Open course. He wanted to reward good ball striking, even off the tee.

And so, key patches of rough were added for the Open, although the course was originally designed without the presence of rough. Davis wanted the bunker in the middle of the 14th fairway to be deeper; he wanted the picturesque 15th hole to play occasionally from 246 yards as well as 165 yards. He added new – and longer – tees on the par-3 third hole.

As the group of nearly 20 people walked off the eighth green in their march around the course on that cold January day, Davis headed off by himself down the hill toward the original driving range. He was searching for a tee position that would require a slightly uphill shot to the par-3 ninth, perhaps the most dramatic hole on the course with its 100 feet of vertical drop to a tumbling green.

Davis could see the hole being played one day as a soaring downhill shot, and another day as a gritty, uphill shot. And he found a spot for a new tee which would provide this disparity. The new tee made it possible to use more of the green, and possible to avoid the hole-in-one location that guided almost every shot to a bowl in the front half of the green.

To allow for the possibility of the 18th hole to be played as both a par-4 and a par-5 during the U.S. Open, renovations began in 2011 to maximize the flexibility in course set-up that Mike Davis had hoped for.

Top: The waste area on the right side of the fairway was extended 100 yards, and now requires a tee shot to carry 280 yards from the back tee when the hole is played as a par-5.

Middle: A cross-bunker on the right side, beyond the newly-enlarged waste area, was extended further into the fairway, creating a hazard for players teeing off the hole's forward tee when the hole is played as a par-4.

Bottom: A large pot bunker was installed in the middle of the fairway 120 yards short of the green, which now asks players to think about their layup second shot when the hole is played as a par-5.

The making of a U.S. Open venue

Chambers Bay opened on June 23, 2007, and when the announcement came in February 2008 that it would be the site of the 2010 U.S. Amateur and the 2015 U.S. Open, not only would the layout go through the normal tweaking performed on any newly-opened course, the modifications would be executed under a microscope as it prepared to host large-scale events.

Most of the renovations took place in the wake of the 2010 U.S. Amateur and prior to the 2013 Washington State Amateur, which was the first significant championship held on the course after the renovations had been completed.

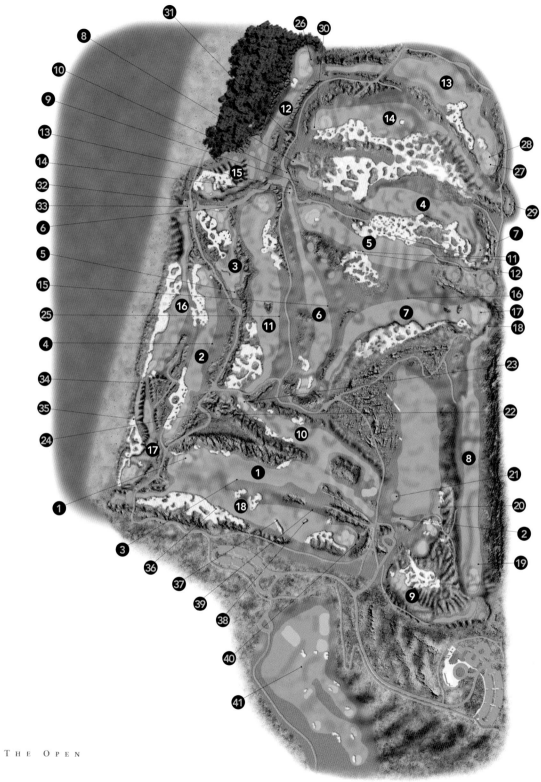

FRONT NINE		
1	Hole 1	Renovated green complex. (2011)
2		New championship tee complex. (2012)
3		Rough line shifted in on the left of fairway. (2012)
4	Hole 2	Rough line shifted in on the right of fairway. (2012)
5	Hole 3	New championship tee complex. (2012)
6		Widened access road for gallery on right side of hole. (2012)
7	Hole 4	New green complex. (2008)
8		New championship tee. (2008)
9		Graded area for concessions on the right side of tee. (2011)
10		Re-routed/widened road for gallery access. (2011)
11	Hole 5	Expanded bunker complex left and right side of fairway. (2012)
12		Removed alternate green on left side. (2012)
13	Hole 6	New championship tee. (2008)
14		New championship tee complex. (2012)
15		Rough line shifted in on left side of fairway. (2012)
16	Hole 7	Rough line shifted in on left side of fairway. (2012)
17		New green complex. (2012)
18	Hole 8	New championship tee complex. (2012)
19		Re-contoured approach and right green surround. (2012)
20	Hole 9	New lower championship tee complex. (2012)

BACK NINE		
21	Hole 10	New championship tee. (2008)
22		Leveled dune on the left side for concession location. (2012)
23		Re-seeded green surface. (2013)
24	Hole 11	New championship tee. (2008)
25		Rough line shifted in on the right side of fairway. (2012)
26	Hole 12	Rough line brought in around right side of green. (2012)
27	Hole 13	New green complex. (2012)
28		Re-seeded green surface. (2013)
29	Hole 14	New championship tee. (2012)
30		Widened walk-off area for improved spectator movement. (2014)
31	Hole 15	New championship tee. (2008)
32	Hole 16	New championship tee. (2014)
33		Added road through tee complex for spectator movement. (2014)
34	Hole 17	Extended lower championship tee. (2008)
35		Removed dune on lower tee to open up view to green. (2012)
36	Hole 18	Extended waste area on right side. (2012)
37		Expanded/deepened cross bunker on right side. (2012)
38		Added pot bunker at 120 yards. (2012)
39		Adjusted rough line and right green surround. (2012)
40		Brought rough line down to green edge. (2013)
41		Added championship practice range. (2008)

During the final round of the Washington State Amateur at Chambers Bay in 2013, held during the same June timeframe and conditions likely to exist for the 2015 Open, the new lower tee on No. 9 was used for the first time in competition.

The shot, that day, was into a strong wind from the southwest, forcing many of the players, the best amateurs in the state, to hit driver off the tee. Shots were sent ballooning into the wind. The demands and feel of the hole were, and are, completely different between the upper and lower tees.

Davis had tipped his hand during the 2010 U.S. Amateur when he used the back tee on No. 15 one day, and a forward tee 100 yards closer to the green on another.

For the final match in the Amateur, he moved the tee on No. 16 up more than 100 yards, making it a drivable par-4, inviting the player behind in the match to go for the green, and the leader to play more sensibly. That hole decided the championship as Peter Uihlein played a hybrid short of the green and David Chung went for the green with a driver and ended up on the side of a dune in knee-deep fescue.

Unlike the Amateur, where the final hole in the championship match proved to be along the Sound at No. 16, the U.S. Open would likely be decided on the 18th, along the remnants of the cement bins, with massive, British Open-style grandstands atop the dunes to the right of the fairway and rows of spectators on the adjoining first hole.

The USGA has usually opted for a long, tough par-4 to finish the U.S. Open. As one official said, "You don't win the U.S. Open with a wedge in your hand."

Davis might put the wedge in play one day, and a fairway metal the next. There's no telling.

It appeared the Open would be played on a par-70 layout, with the normally par-5 fourth and 13th holes being played as par-4s.

For the climactic 18th hole, Davis wanted the waste area expanded off the tee, and it was, by nearly 100 yards, forcing players keeping to the right to carry 280 yards or more with their tee shots.

Avoiding the waste area brought the large fairway bunkers on the left into play. A bunker on the right side was extended into the fairway to catch errant shots flying too far over the waste area.

Then came the addition by Davis of a deep pot bunker some 120 yards short of the huge, three-level green. Davis wanted the bunker deep enough that only the world's very best players might be able to reach the green from its depths.

On their tour on that January day, Davis and Jones each stepped into the newly-dug pot bunker, vanishing from sight. Each emerged smiling, Davis giving a thumbs up, Jones a thumbs down.

The bunker interrupted the final strains of Jones' sandy symphony. It was understandable he didn't want it. But because this was the U.S. Open, and because Davis didn't want a lazy layup shot when the hole was played as a par-5, and because he was the most powerful man in golf, Davis prevailed.

The middle-of-the-fairway pot bunker – to be avoided at all costs – is a conversation piece if nothing else. Like the great bunkers at the Old Course at St. Andrews, the 10-foot deep hole was quickly given a nickname: Chambers Basement, so named by the course's sardonic caddies.

For a time, Davis talked about adding a bunker behind the green to take away the backboard effect that delights amateurs, but decided the finishing hole was tough enough.

"There are hole locations on that green that can only be reached with a wedge shot," he said. "The possibilities are endless."

In time, Chambers Bay will be remembered for great shots and great competitions, not its unlikely beginnings and longshot label.

After John Ladenburg's tenure as head of Pierce County had come and gone, he ran for a spot on the state's Supreme Court. He never had a chance.

"You know," he said, "I had never lost an election in my life, but this time I didn't even carry my home district."

He believed his unpopularity could be traced directly to the money spent by taxpayers to build Chambers Bay and his quixotic quest for the U.S. Open.

"I'd do it over again in a heartbeat," he said. "People don't understand now, but they will."

And should for years to come. ✳

Opposite: Wanting no easy lay-up second shot on the 18th hole when it's played as a par-5, Mike Davis ordered the addition of a 10-foot deep bunker in the middle of the fairway some 120 yards short of the green. Here he inspects the view, or lack thereof, shortly after its construction in 2012.

The Shape of Things to Come

The fate, and the face, of Chambers Bay took a turn on that cold day in January of 2011, when Robert Trent Jones Jr. and Bruce Charlton, the course's architects, walked the course with USGA Executive Director Mike Davis and his team of specialists from both inside and outside the ropes.

In discussing the necessary renovations in the wake of the 2010 U.S. Amateur, it wasn't Davis versus Jones, although at times it could have been.

The renovations to the course were a collaborative effort, performed in a civil manner by two giants who had enormous respect for each other. In the weeks and months that followed that January day, their correspondence shows the breadth of their understanding of the significant journey they were on together, displayed with gravity and with humor.

(Unknown date, time)
Mike: Bob and Bruce, thanks for a great half-day. I am elated with the changes. I hope you are too. Thanks for your support and guidance! Mike

(Unknown date, time)
Bobby: Thank you, Mike, for your continued support and creative insights. We too are happy with the work inside the ropes. Brother Jones (Reg) needs to be careful: once a hard surface always a hard surface on a golf course, also cost is a factor as you and the county know. More aesthetically important is having the time for Ed to re-craft the Chambers Bay dune-look by tying all the disturbed areas back together. Beauty is its own pleasure. Thanks again for your effort to be here. Everyone appreciates your comments. We will try to make them a reality. Bob

(Unknown date, time)
Mike: Thanks Bob. You are so right; there's a happy balance between doing what is right for this (and the next!) Open and doing what is right for everyday play. Thanks again for all your support, creativeness and wisdom. Best, Mike

October 15, 2012 – 6:25 A.M.
Bobby: Played Chambers Bay yesterday. Thought I was still in Scotland. Maybe Turnberry. The refinements and turf care is 80 percent there. Talked to serious player-caddies and others. Most analysis is very positive. A general concern is that No. 18 is getting too busy. Not about your bunker, but trying to be both a par-5 and a par-4 at the same time…..A suggestion: play 18 as a par-4 on Sunday, lower the hump in front slightly to reveal several flagstick options for you to choose from. Let's talk. Bob

October 15, 2012 – 7:53 A.M.
Mike: Wonderful as always to hear from you. I am sorry I missed you in St. Andrews. While I still like the idea of playing hole 18 as a par-4 and 5 (in large part because of your wonderfully flexible design), I do think what you mention about the hump has very good merit. We should explore….. Thanks again for everything, Bob. All the best, Mike

November 6, 2012 – 12:07 P.M.
Mike: By the way, I did have a good discussion with Matt A and Larry G. They have convinced me that we can absolutely grow rough on the backstop behind 18 green. I am fine if we do that and therefore do not disturb the area. Best, Mike

Bobby: Thanks Mike. You are my favorite golf thinker and chess player. Best always, Bob

THE OPEN

143

Are there any better finishing holes? Anywhere?

Where History Is Made

COMING OFF THE GREEN ON NO. 14 AT CHAMBERS BAY and beginning the 100-yard walk to the tee at No. 15, the sense of anticipation that has been simmering all through the back nine comes to the surface and lightens your step. The entire round has been leading to this moment, to this last stretch of holes. The work and effort in playing the round to this point is about to be rewarded with unbounded beauty, terrific scenery, marvelous golf course architecture and a supreme test of mental and physical ability.

Are there any better finishing holes? Anywhere?

The drop-down to the water's level, with the ferries plying Puget Sound, itself carved by glaciers in a previous epoch, to McNeil and Anderson Islands with the silhouette of the Olympic Mountains in the background; the 10,000 years of human history who have walked this land; the railroad tracks that now transfer people and industry from city to city; and finally the relics of a hundred years of sand and gravel mining from a mighty endeavor in days gone by – all of this, every bit of it, is the background as an ancient game is played over this piece of Earth.

Can holes be considered great when they have not been tested by great players in great championships? But this is all now being changed and validated.

The most recognizable hole on the course, No. 15 is the great short par-3 that every great course must have. And this one with the iconic Lone Fir silhouetted against the waters of Puget Sound.

With the tees moved up in the final match of the 2010 U.S. Amateur to make it a risk-reward drivable par-4, No. 16 played to perfection as it became the deciding hole in the match as David Chung made one last effort in his comeback before bowing to champion Peter Uihlein.

With its multi-leveled teeing grounds and undulating green, No. 17 is a muscular and terrifying par-3 that lives up to its nickname, "Derailed," as it threatens to ruin round after round. During the 2013 Washington State Amateur, this hole had the highest scoring average in relation to par.

Byeong-Hun An, the 2009 U.S. Amateur champion attempting to defend his title at Chambers Bay in 2010, lost on No. 18, the final hole of his semifinal match against Chung, when he couldn't extricate himself from the wispy grass inside a greenside bunker, bowing to the vagaries and randomness of links golf.

And now a U.S. Open, and the attempt at identifying the game's greatest players.

The shots that are required on the four finishing holes at Chambers Bay – how purely they must be struck, the imagination with which they must be visualized, their variety, and the backdrop in which they will be played – are the best kind of work, because they ask you to work as if at play.

And play you will.

No. 15 - "Lone Fir"
Par 3

Every great course has a great short par-3. There is something inherently frightening about this beautiful little golf hole. The elevated teeing grounds somehow prevent a golfer from ever really letting the ball go, from putting it up into the air and giving it away to the whims of the wind coming in off the water.

The backstops on the left and back of the green provide forgiving bailout areas, while a hole location on the right side offers no margin for error.

And for those special occasions, those memorable events, those national championships, a teeing ground has been added beyond the adjacent 12th tee across the path and up on top of a dune. Located in the lower-left of the photo, the player must hit a tee shot across the teeing ground of No. 12. Measuring 246 yards from this newly added tee, this beautiful little hole becomes beautifully long.

No. 16 - "Beached"
Par 4

Perhaps the best hole on the golf course, the par-4 16th is the beauty and the beast of Chambers Bay, and a pivotal hole in any round.

First of all, it breaks your concentration. Standing in the shadow of the Lone Fir, with the teeing area (and particularly the new championship tees) nearly cantilevered over the railroad tracks, the rumbling freight train itself, the beach below and the ferries slipping out to the islands, there is so much to see and do.

Cleaved by the architects from a shelf of sand 30 feet tall, the entire fairway heaves and slopes from left to right toward a gaping waste area that runs the entire length of the right side. With considerable room left, the tee shot can easily avoid the waste area, but therein lies the challenge of the hole. Drives hit left present an extremely difficult – if not impossible – second shot. The green simply refuses to accommodate shots coming in from the left, particularly if the flag is located in the back-right narrow thumb, with a bunker so close that well-meaning putts have rolled into it.

The hole can be the toughest on the course when a storm brings a strong southerly wind. Or it can be drivable in the prevailing north wind if the tees are moved forward.

No. 17 - "Derailed"
Par 3

This, really, is more than a golf hole. This is where cultures have collided and are now finally at peace. It is at this point, from this pier, where industry had shipped gravel for over a hundred years; and it is at this point that human beings have walked for over 10,000 years, gazing at the islands across the water and the mountains in the distance. And on these railroad tracks were brought the building blocks of cities up and down the West Coast. And now a public walkway runs along the length of the hole on the left side, where golfers and non-golfers enjoy the fruits of industry and philosophy.

And the hole itself? When played from the lower, longer teeing grounds, set down below the dune and near the railroad tracks, this par-3 gives the illusion of simultaneously being cramped and wide open.

With the wind pushing in from right to left off the water, the tee shot will have to start out almost over the railroad tracks, with the ball being brought back to one of the wilder greens on the course. To be able to stop a ball on the back-right tier hole location under almost any weather condition and under almost any pressure condition will require a significant reservoir of skill and bravery.

No. 18 - "Tahoma"
Par 5

To really understand a great finishing hole you must read it from back to front – from green to tee – and the green on the 18th at Chambers Bay is a lumpy minefield of heroes and heartbreak.

Because it was designed as a par-5, there are hole locations on the sides and tops of mounds that can be held only with a well-struck wedge.

But for the Open, the 18th will be played as both a par-4 and a par-5, likely in unprecedented fashion, alternating daily depending on the wind and the whims of the USGA's Mike Davis.

As a par-5, the tee backs up almost into Puget Sound, 604 yards from the green. A tee shot down the right side of the fairway must carry 280 yards to clear an expanded waste area – Davis' doing – while anything hit left faces a sandy fate in any number of bunkers.

The second shot on the par-5, if going for the green, will be to a very difficult hole location. Even a lay-up shot will be perilous, as Davis has added a 10-foot deep pot bunker in the middle of the fairway some 120 yards short of the green that would almost surely mean a dropped shot.

Played as a par-4, the tee shot would face a different set of challenges. Indeed, a drive hit over the bunkers on the left could bound down into a nasty bunker projecting out into the fairway from the right.

The challenge for Davis will be to find a hole location that can handle a 3-iron approach shot on the par-4. The challenge for the greatest players in the world will be to hit it.

Golf's Roots in the Pacific Northwest Run Deep

BY JEFF SHELLEY

The 2015 U.S. Open will bring thousands of visitors to the Pacific Northwest along with millions of television viewers worldwide for what is assuredly the largest sporting event ever held in the region. It will be a landmark occasion for America's upper-left-hand corner, which has made underrated but profound contributions to the great game of golf for well over a century.

Indeed, the sport has extensive roots in the Northwest, perhaps as deep as any place in North America. Michael Riste, curator of the BC Golf House in Vancouver, has researched a primitive course built beside Puget Sound near Steilacoom – just south of Chambers Bay – and played by Scotsmen working at a Hudson's Bay Company outpost there in 1846 and 1847.

"Wherever the Scots went in the world, the first thing they did was build a golf course," Riste says with assurance.

Based on newspaper accounts, the earliest "official" courses were built in the 1880s by Scottish immigrants in Victoria and Vancouver, B.C., and in Tacoma and along Oregon's coast in Gearhart. In 1892, Gearhart Golf Links was formed, becoming the first organized club west of the Mississippi River. Five years after the United States Golf Association was founded in 1894, the Pacific Northwest Golf Association was launched, making it the fifth-oldest golf association in North America.

One of Northwest golf's germinators, Alexander Baillie, a transplanted Scot who founded Tacoma Country & Golf Club in 1894 and was believed to be playing golf in Washington state as early as 1885, first brought golf clubs to the region for sale (imported by Baillie's employer, Balfour, Guthrie & Co.) in the late 1800s.

Josiah Collins – a founder of historic Seattle Golf Club – described the occasion in a 1937 interview: "The customs agent, when told they were golf clubs, said he had never heard of the game. After having it described to him by Mr. Baillie, the agent said: 'Well, I'll enter them as garden tools. You'll probably dig up the ground anyway.'"

Thus were sown the modest seeds of golf in the Northwest, which has produced influential golfers and personalities, great courses and big-time tournaments. One of the game's most illustrious early-day golfers, "Long Jim" Barnes, had a local connection. The Cornishman arrived in America in 1906 and made stops in Spokane (where he designed Spokane Country Club's first nine holes) and Tacoma. Before leaving for the East Coast in 1914, Barnes honed his vaunted game by winning four Northwest Open titles. He went on to win the first two PGA Championships, 1921 U.S. Open (by nine strokes over Walter Hagen) and 1925 British Open.

After winning the 1902 Western Amateur and two straight U.S. Amateurs in 1904 and '05, Chicago native H. Chandler Egan moved west to Medford, Ore. in 1911, where he soon formed a partnership with seminal golf architect Alister MacKenzie. The pair redesigned Pebble Beach Golf Links in advance of the first USGA national championship held on the West Coast, the 1929 U.S. Amateur. Before his premature death at age 51 in 1936, Egan created several of the Northwest's landmark courses, including Eugene Country Club, Rogue Valley Country Club and Eastmoreland in Oregon, and Indian Canyon and West Seattle in Washington.

Another important golf architect with a home in the neighborhood was Arthur Vernon Macan, who many modern-day observers consider a trailblazer in his construction of greens and creation of courses that challenged low-handicappers while making them accessible for average players. The Victoria-based Macan, who lost his lower-left leg during the Battle of Vimy Ridge in World War I but still kept a 6-handicap afterward, crafted such superb layouts as Columbia Edgewater in Portland, Fircrest near Tacoma, Royal Colwood in Victoria, and Manito in Spokane.

In 1915, Robert Johnstone, also a Scottish immigrant and a longtime golf professional at Seattle Golf Club, designed Jefferson Park in Seattle, the Northwest's first municipal course and a future training ground for 1992 Masters champion and Emerald City native Fred Couples.

Some of the region's great players include George Von Elm, Dr. Oscar F. Willing and Don Moe, who were teammates of Bobby Jones and Francis Ouimet on America's victorious 1930 Walker Cup team. Olympia's Bud Ward won two U.S. Amateur and three Western Amateur titles before becoming a noted instructor in California, helping, among many others, seven-time USGA champion Anne Sander of Seattle to her first two U.S. Women's Amateur titles.

Also on the list is Jack Westland, who lost in the finals of the 1931 U.S. Amateur to Ouimet but, 21 years later, at age 46, became the oldest golfer ever to win the coveted Havemeyer Trophy, with the Amateur being held that year, 1952, at Seattle Golf Club. A year after his Amateur victory, Westland began a 12-year stretch as a member of the U.S. House of Representatives.

The first major held in the Northwest was the 1944 PGA Championship, played at Spokane's Manito Golf & Country Club (in an epic 1-up upset, Bob Hamilton beat Byron Nelson). Two years later, the PGA Championship returned to the region, at Portland Golf Club. The Rose City event was spearheaded by a local grocer, Robert Hudson, and won by Ben Hogan. During that tournament, the Golf Writers Association of America was founded by the *Chicago Tribune's* Charles Bartlett, Associated Press editor Russ Newland, and *Oregon Journal* sports editor George Bertz in an empty ice-cream stand beside the 18th green. Hudson also played a major role in resuscitating the Ryder Cup, personally funding the first post-war matches, held in 1947 at Portland Golf Club.

The U.S. Women's Amateur was owned by Seattle-area golfers over a 13-year period in the 1950s and '60s. Pat (Lesser) Harbottle (1955), JoAnne (Gunderson) Carner (1957, '60, '62, '66 and '68) and Sander (1958, '61 and '63) ruled the national women's golf championship with nine victories.

With eight overall national titles (she also won the 1956 U.S. Girls' Junior and the 1971 and 1976 U.S. Women's Opens), Carner is tied for second on the USGA's all-time winners list with Jack Nicklaus and only one behind Tiger Woods and Jones, while Sander's seven are tied for third with Carol Semple Thompson. Two of Woods' titles came in the Northwest – the 1993 U.S. Junior Amateur at Waverley Country Club and his third U.S. Amateur victory in 1996 at Pumpkin Ridge, both venues being located in the Portland area.

In addition to Couples, other recent Northwesterners who went on to great things on the national stage include Bill Wright (the first African-American winner of a USGA championship – the 1959 U.S. Amateur Public Links), Peter Jacobsen, Jim McLean, Bill Sander, Rick Fehr, Doug Roxburgh, Dave Barr, Ken Still, Richard Zokol, John Fought, Don Bies, Jo Ann Washam, Jim Nelford and current touring pros Ben Crane, Robert Garrigus, Bob Gilder, Andres Gonzales, Jeff Gove, Alex Prugh, Michael Putnam, Mike Reid, Kirk Triplett, Jim Rutledge, Mark Wiebe, Kyle Stanley, Ryan Moore, Jimin Kang, Richard H. Lee, James Lepp, Wendy Ward, Kim Welch and Paige Mackenzie.

Many players from the Northwest are members of the World Golf Hall of Fame, Canadian Golf Hall of Fame, Golf Hall of Fame of BC and the Pacific Northwest Golf Hall of Fame.

Recent No. 1-ranked amateurs in the world include Chris Williams, Nick Taylor and Cheng-Tsung Pan, all of whom starred on the University of Washington men's golf team. John Bodenhamer, the longtime executive director of the PNGA and Washington State Golf Association, and the 1981 Washington State Amateur champion, is now the USGA's senior managing director of rules, competitions and equipment standards.

So, despite many visitors and viewers experiencing golf in the beautiful Pacific Northwest for the first time during the 2015 U.S. Open at glorious Chambers Bay, golf has been an integral part of the region's culture for well over a century.

Jeff Shelley is the author of three editions of the book, "Golf Courses of the Pacific Northwest," co-founder of the Northwest Golf Media Association, co-author and publisher of "Championships & Friendships: The First 100 Years of the Pacific Northwest Golf Association," and longtime editorial director of Cybergolf.com.

Significant Championships Held in the Pacific Northwest

U.S. Open

2015   Chambers Bay – University Place, Wash.

PGA Championship

1998   Sahalee Country Club – Sammamish, Wash.
1946   Portland Golf Club – Portland, Ore.
1944   Manito Golf & Country Club – Spokane, Wash.

Canadian Open

2011   Shaughnessy Golf & Country Club – Vancouver, B.C.
2005   Shaughnessy Golf & Country Club – Vancouver, B.C.
1966   Shaughnessy Golf & Country Club – Vancouver, B.C.
1954   Point Grey Golf & Country Club – Vancouver, B.C.
1948   Shaughnessy Golf & Country Club – Vancouver, B.C.

U.S. Senior Open

2010   Sahalee Country Club – Sammamish, Wash.
1982   Portland Golf Club – Portland, Ore.

U.S. Women's Open

2003   Pumpkin Ridge Golf Club, Witch Hollow – North Plains, Ore.
1997   Pumpkin Ridge Golf Club, Witch Hollow – North Plains, Ore.
1946   Spokane Country Club – Spokane, Wash.

Ryder Cup

1947   Portland Golf Club – Portland, Ore.

Walker Cup

1961   Seattle Golf Club – Seattle, Wash.

Curtis Cup

2006   Bandon Dunes Golf Resort – Bandon, Ore.

U.S. Amateur

2010   Chambers Bay – University Place, Wash.
1996   Pumpkin Ridge Golf Club, Witch Hollow – North Plains, Ore.
1970   Waverley Country Club – Portland, Ore.
1952   Seattle Golf Club – Seattle, Wash.
1937   Alderwood Country Club – Portland, Ore.

U.S. Women's Amateur

2015   Portland Golf Club – Portland, Ore.
2008   Eugene Country Club – Eugene, Ore.
2006   Pumpkin Ridge Golf Club, Witch Hollow – North Plains, Ore.
2000   Waverley Country Club – Portland, Ore.
1984   Broadmoor Golf Club – Seattle, Wash.
1981   Waverley Country Club – Portland, Ore.
1974   Broadmoor Golf Club – Seattle, Wash.
1961   Tacoma Country & Golf Club – Lakewood, Wash.
1952   Waverley Country Club – Portland, Ore.

U.S. Mid-Amateur

2007   Bandon Dunes Golf Resort – Bandon, Ore.
1993   Eugene Country Club – Eugene, Ore.

U.S. Women's Mid-Amateur

2002	Eugene Country Club – Eugene, Ore.
1994	Tacoma Country & Golf Club – Lakewood, Wash.

U.S. Senior Amateur

1999	Portland Golf Club – Portland, Ore.
1981	Seattle Golf Club – Seattle, Wash.
1964	Waverley Country Club – Portland, Ore.

U.S. Senior Women's Amateur

2007	Sunriver Resort, Meadows – Sunriver, Ore.
1996	Broadmoor Golf Club – Seattle, Wash.
1984	Tacoma Country & Golf Club – Lakewood, Wash.

U.S. Amateur Public Links

2011	Bandon Dunes Golf Resort – Bandon, Ore.
2006	Gold Mountain Golf Club, Olympic – Bremerton, Wash.
2000	Heron Lakes Golf Club, Great Blue – Portland, Ore.
1990	Eastmoreland Golf Course – Portland, Ore.
1984	Indian Canyon Golf Course – Spokane, Wash.
1979	West Delta Golf Course – Portland, Ore.
1967	Jefferson Park Golf Course – Seattle, Wash.
1953	West Seattle Golf Course – Seattle, Wash.
1941	Indian Canyon Golf Course – Spokane, Wash.
1933	Eastmoreland Golf Course – Portland, Ore.

U.S. Women's Amateur Public Links

2014	The Home Course – DuPont, Wash.
2011	Bandon Dunes Golf Resort – Bandon, Ore.
2002	Sunriver Resort, Meadows – Sunriver, Ore.
1989	Indian Canyon Golf Course – Spokane, Wash.
1981	Emerald Valley Golf Club – Creswell, Ore.

U.S. Women's Amateur Four-Ball

2015	Bandon Dunes Golf Resort – Bandon, Ore.

U.S. Junior Amateur

2011	Gold Mountain Golf Club, Olympic – Bremerton, Wash.
2000	Pumpkin Ridge Golf Club, Ghost Creek – North Plains, Ore.
1993	Waverley Country Club – Portland, Ore.
1969	Spokane Country Club – Spokane, Wash.
1964	Eugene Country Club – Eugene, Ore.

U.S. Girls' Junior

2007	Tacoma Country & Golf Club – Lakewood, Wash.
2005	BanBury Golf Course – Eagle, Idaho
2000	Pumpkin Ridge Golf Club, Ghost Creek – North Plains, Ore.
1984	Mill Creek Country Club – Mill Creek, Wash.
1981	Illahe Hills Country Club – Salem, Ore.
1974	Columbia Edgewater Country Club – Portland, Ore.
1961	Broadmoor Golf Club – Seattle, Wash.

HOLE	Championship 78.1/146	Navy 75.6/139	Sand 72.4/135	White (M) 70.2/127 (W) 76.2/137	Handicap	Par	Handicap	Blue 71.5/128
1	600	559	501	465	3	5	3	436
2	404	395	365	337	13	4	11	301
3	193	167	145	130	17	3	17	111
4	568	530	480	424	5	5	7	347
5	490	465	441	423	9	4	9	323
6	498	418	369	315	11	4	13	283
7	508	482	449	435	7	4	5	415
8	614	557	523	488	1	5	15	441
9	227/220	227	202	168	15	3	15	132
OUT	4102/4095	3800	3475	3185		37		2789
10	436	398	360	330	10	4	8	311
11	537	457	425	402	8	4	4	378
12	304	281	262	246	14	4	14	219
13	534	485	453	437	2	4	6	348
14	546	496	407	383	6	4	10	309
15	246/172	139	116	103	18	3	16	91
16	425	396	359	323	12	4	12	279
17	206	172	142	119	16	3	18	92
18	604	541	514	487	4	5	2	462
IN	3838/3764	3365	3038	2830		35		2489
TOTAL	7940/7859	7165	6513	6015		72		5278

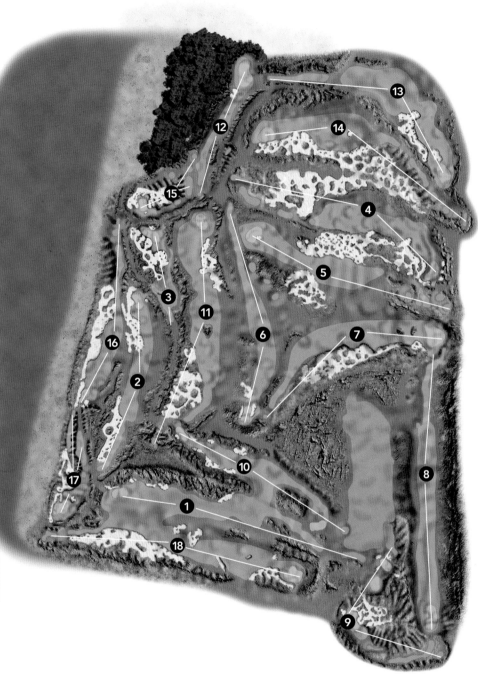

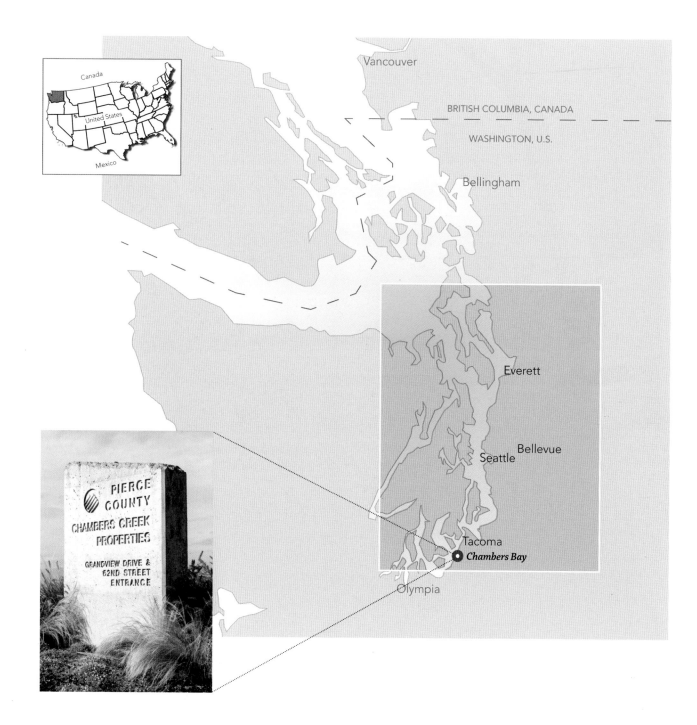

Canada

United States

Mexico

Vancouver

BRITISH COLUMBIA, CANADA

WASHINGTON, U.S.

Bellingham

Everett

Bellevue

Seattle

Tacoma

Chambers Bay

Olympia

PIERCE COUNTY

CHAMBERS CREEK PROPERTIES

GRANDVIEW DRIVE & 62ND STREET ENTRANCE

Acknowledgements

Books of this kind, with so many moving parts, do not happen by themselves, nor do they happen with one or two people stumbling around in the darkness. In the three years of preparing this project, there were many from whose well we drew the cool, clear waters of experience, information and insight.

Matt Allen – The general manager of Chambers Bay who, in a dimly-lit Mexican restaurant in Tacoma on a dark winter's day, over tortilla chips and salsa, first suggested the idea for this book; and whose generosity of access and time lit the path on which we would walk. Without Matt, this book would not have happened.

Bruce Charlton – The president of Robert Trent Jones II, and the lead architect of Chambers Bay. His enthusiasm for his work spilled over into his enthusiasm in answering our questions (fortunately for us).

Trent Jones – The director of branding and media at Robert Trent Jones II. He opened the vaults and shared with us the creativity and the minds of the architects who laid their hands upon an abandoned gravel pit and made it shine.

John Ladenburg – If we wanted the truth, whether we liked the answer or not, we asked John.

Tony Tipton – Director of the Parks and Recreation Department for Pierce County, Tony has seen the entire progression of the property, and was an invaluable resource of information.

Connie Perry – The longtime executive secretary at the Pierce County Executive's office. Whenever we came to a dead end, Connie always had the answers.

Joe Scorcio – The deputy public works director for Pierce County during the building of Chambers Bay. It was Joe who offered up his cache of historical photos when this book was still just an idea.

Jamie Fay – The director of marketing and assistant general manager at Chambers Bay who opened many doors, even the ones we didn't know we wanted to go through yet.

Brian Simpson – The director of client services at Chambers Bay. He was there, then was gone, and then came back in a big way.

Hunter George – The communications director for Pierce County. Always available, always positive, always generous with his time and ideas.

Ron Bellamy – The former sports editor and columnist for the *Eugene* (Ore.) *Register-Guard*, whose cool head talked us away from many ledges.

Troy Andrew – The CEO and executive director of the Pacific Northwest Golf Association and Washington State Golf Association. He never questioned anything we were doing, and for that display of trust was freely given all the answers.

Laurie Watson – The external relations and media manager of St. Andrews Links Trust in Scotland, who allowed us to share with them in spreading the gospel of the ancient game.

Tony Dear – For his contributions to chapter seven. He grew up in England playing the classic links of the UK, but the Northwest now claims this award-winning golf writer as its own.

Abell Smith – The webmaster for the Pacific Northwest Golf Association, for his creativity, insights, eye for detail, and for his ability to keep finding things for us to do (and they were always the right things).

Jeff Shelley – The author and publisher of several regional golf books, whose early advice pointed us in the right direction.

Jay Blasi – One of the on-site project architects of Chambers Bay while he was with Robert Trent Jones II. Jay loves this golf course, and was always available to share the experience of this first love.

Dick Ferguson – For the photos he shot (a few of which are featured in this book) while working for Pierce County as manager of media and community relations during the building of Chambers Bay. Dick knew, even then, he was witnessing something special.

Bruce Christy – The director of golf at White Horse Golf Club in Kingston, Wash., who gave us work space in his clubhouse and offered us milk and cookies as well as caffeinated products.

Andrea Clay – The recreation supervisor for Pierce County, who generously shared her file of photos of public events held at Chambers Creek Properties.

Kacie Bray – The director of marketing for the Washington State Golf Association, who helped two old guys look presentable.

Photo Credits

Most of the photography is the work of two contributors, who also assisted with photo editing.

Rob Perry
robperry.com

In 1994, Rob Perry began his photography career after graduating from Brooks Institute of Photography in Santa Barbara, Calif. Combining his passion for the game of golf and eye for photography, he built his career by capturing the architectural design and natural beauty of golf courses around the Northwest and beyond. His work has been featured in numerous national publications, including *Golf Magazine*, *Golf Digest*, *Links* magazine, *Time* magazine and *Pacific Northwest Golfer* magazine. Rob's work has also been featured in the USGA annual calendar and the Nicklaus Golf calendar, as well as in the books "Golf Architecture – A Worldwide Perspective," *Golf Magazine's* "Top 100 Courses You Can Play," the Rolex "World's Top 1000 Golf Courses" and "Golf Courses of the World," among many others.

Rob served for several years as vice president of the Northwest Golf Media Association.

Jason Mercio
merciophotography.com

For Jason Mercio, the assignment of looking at Chambers Bay in a different light was a perfect marriage of his love of the outdoors and background in interior and architectural photography.

A native of Buffalo, N.Y., Jason has done extensive real estate photography in Denver and now Seattle. He attended West Virginia University before moving westward.

His sideline photography of the natural architectural marvels of the national parks in Utah – Bryce Canyon, Arches and Canyonlands – is stunning. Since arriving in Seattle in 2008, he has focused his love of outdoor photography on the Oregon Coast.

Until Chambers Bay came along.

Chris Anderson, another major contributor
2-chris-anderson.artistwebsites.com

GeoEngineers, Inc.: 96L

MillerBrown Photography: 139, 154

National Park Service: 75M

Pacific Northwest Golf Association: 30RT, 30RB, 33, 35R, 122B

Pierce County: 8-9T, 8-9B, 12, 21, 25TL, 25BL, 25R, 31, 40, 46L, 47, 48L, 48R, 49, 50T, 50B, 51, 52, 54, 59R, 60T, 62, 63, 64, 66, 82, 84, 86, 87, 90, 91B, 94B, 95, 99L, 124R

Pierce County Department of Public Works: 60B, 70, 73, 74LB, 76R

Pierce County Executive Office: 38L-R, 39L-R, 44B, 125

Robert Trent Jones Licensing Group: 20, 91TL, 91TR, 92L, 92R, 94T, 97

Steilacoom Historical Society: 72L, 72R

Tacoma Public Library: 7, 68, 74LT, 74R, 77

University of St. Andrews Library: 24TL, 24BL

USGA Museum: 133

USGA/John Mummert: 17, 102, 121, back cover dust jacket

Mark Alexander: 32, 35L

Chris Anderson: 3, 16, 61, 78, 79, 104, 130

Jay Blasi: 89

Bill Brisky: 24R

Tom Cade: 58, 67L, 108, 109, 112, 116, 117L, 119L, 122L, 122T, 123 all, 124L, 128, 132T, 135L, 135R, 136T, 158L

Dick Durrance II: 13

John Ladenburg: 44T

Joe Mabel: 75T, 75B

Jeff Marsh: 117R, 120T, 120B

Jason Mercio: 4, 18, 22, 26, 42, 45, 46R, 59L, 65, 67R, 76L, 80-81, 99R, 107, 111, 136B, 137, 138 all, 146, 148, 156

Martin Miller: 14, 15, 34

Blaine Newnham: 88, 141, 142 all, 143, 158R

Lisa Newnham: 159L

Rob Perry: 10-11, 28, 37, 93, 96R, 98, 100, 101, 106, 110, 114, 118, 119R, 126, 127, 132B, 134, 147, 149, 151, 160, front cover dust jacket

Susan Terry: 159R

Corky Trewin: 56T, 56B

Mark Ursino: 30L

Neal Wolbert: 57 all

About the Author

Blaine Newnham, author

Infatuated both by links golf and the Northwest, Blaine's work on "America's St. Andrews" is a natural progression in the arc of his career and his life. He has played the great courses of the British Isles, from St. Andrews and Royal Dornoch in Scotland, to Royal Porthcawl in Wales, to Lahinch and Ballybunion in Ireland. He has authored two previous books, "The Running Experience" and Barnes & Nobles' "Golf Basics."

Blaine has played golf for 60 years and covered it for 50. His career as a journalist began in the San Francisco Bay area, covering the NFL's Oakland Raiders for the *Oakland Tribune*. It was during his tenure there that he walked 18 holes in the shadow of Ben Hogan during the 1966 U.S. Open at the Olympic Club.

He later was a sports editor and columnist for 11 years with Oregon's *Eugene Register-Guard*, and an associate editor and sports columnist for *The Seattle Times* for 23 years. He is a featured writer in *Pacific Northwest Golfer* magazine and Cybergolf.com, as well as *Golfweek* magazine.

As Blaine turned to writing more about golf during his years at the newspapers, he covered seven Masters, seven U.S. Opens and three British Opens. He covered the four consecutive majors that Tiger Woods won, and

was there to watch Payne Stewart's par putt to win the 1999 U.S. Open at Pinehurst. He also covered five Olympic Games – Mexico City, Munich, Los Angeles, Seoul and Athens – before retiring in 2005 from the *Times*.

In 2005, Blaine received the Distinguished Service Award from the Northwest Golf Media Association, and is a regular member of the Golf Writers Association of America. He and his wife, Joanna, live in Indianola, Wash., where the Dungeness crabs outnumber the people.

Tom Cade, editor and publisher

Tom is the editor of *Pacific Northwest Golfer* magazine, which is published by the Pacific Northwest Golf Association (PNGA). He is also the senior director of communications for the PNGA and the Washington State Golf Association. From 2010-2015 he served as president of the Northwest Golf Media Association, for which he also served as managing director in 2005-2006, and is a regular member of the Golf Writers Association of America. He lives north of Seattle on a small farm, where he tends to a small but enthusiastic herd of Pygmy goats.

Art Direction and Design

Marilyn B. Esguerra

For over 20 years Marilyn has been the behind-the-scenes creative force for numerous golf clubs, courses, resorts and events throughout the Pacific Northwest, with her work being seen in many logos, ad campaigns, collateral material and websites of the region's golf community. She has been the art director and designer for *Pacific Northwest Golfer* magazine, the region's premier golf publication, since 2003.

Marilyn has designed and produced other large-scale coffee table books in her role as art director for Philips Publishing Group in Seattle, Wash., for which she also serves as lead designer of several quarterly magazines.